T0270585

Praise for
ONE GENERATION AWAY

"We are all concerned about the future of America. Were every young student as engaged and patriotic as Brilyn, we would have our every fear assuaged. His book is timely, necessary, and will inspire the newest generation of voters, upon which the future of this great country depends."
—**Candace Owens,** *conservative commentator*

"I often say the future of America lies in the hands of young patriots who are willing to carry the torch of liberty and freedom. My friend Brilyn, one of those patriots, has delivered a rallying cry to his generation and many to come that this nation is worth fighting for. While President Reagan's wise words may have been a warning, they were also a challenge. This book gives me hope that challenge has been accepted."
—**Dr. Ben Carson,** *former secretary of the United States Department of Housing and Urban Development*

"Brilyn's important message will no doubt inspire more young leaders like him to get off the sidelines and step into their arena. It's time for the next generation of conservatives to step up in order to preserve the American Dream and save our country."
—**Katie Boyd Britt,** *Republican United States senator from Alabama*

"Brilyn is exactly the type of young patriot who should and will be leading our next generation of voters. He understands how important this generation is to the future of our country and he lays out how to effectively reach them!"

—**Sean Spicer,** *former White House press secretary*

"I'm far more concerned about the world my seven grandchildren will live in than the one I've experienced because there are genuine threats to the very existence of our free republic from forces that show no respect to the Constitution we all live under. It's why Brilyn Hollyhand's timely message *One Generation Away: Why Now Is the Time to Restore American Freedom* is a must-read for those who wonder if America will survive the relentless assault on our underlying Judeo-Christian foundations. Brilyn's message and its call to action deserves your attention!"

—**Mike Huckabee,** *former governor of Arkansas*

"'Freedom is never more than one generation away from Extinction.' This is one of my favorite quotes from former President Ronald Reagan, who I had the privilege to know personally. My father, Eugene Greenwood, joined the Navy the day following the bombing of Pearl Harbor. It was a shock that rocked the United Sates and tested our resolve. I was raised by this nation's 'greatest generation' and remember the sacrifice of all who served. The phrase 'freedom isn't free' is absolutely true, but it concerns me that for so many, it's taken for granted. In this book, this brilliant young man, Brilyn Hollyhand, points out the obvious. Freedom is not free, and every generation has a responsibility to defend it. I've always believed that America's best days are ahead of us. I hope that

Brilyn's youthful enthusiasm will inspire his generation and the next to embrace that ideal."

—**Lee Greenwood,** *Grammy Award–winning and multi-platinum recording artist*

"In what seems to be a declining culture, Brilyn's book should give all Americans hope. After reading *One Generation Away: Why Now Is the Time to Restore American Freedom,* you will walk away feeling equipped with the mindset and resources necessary to restore morality and sanity to this once-united nation. This book isn't just for conservatives; it's for anyone who wants to see a thriving America once again!"

—**Riley Gaines,** *twelve-time NCAA all-American swimmer*

ONE GENERATION AWAY

ONE GENERATION AWAY

WHY NOW IS THE TIME TO
RESTORE
AMERICAN
FREEDOM

BRILYN HOLLYHAND

Since 1947
REGNERY
An Imprint of Skyhorse Publishing, Inc.

All Scripture quotations, unless otherwise indicated, are taken from the Holy Bible, New International Version®, NIV®. Copyright © 1973, 1978, 1984, 2011 by Biblica, Inc.® Used by permission of Zondervan. All rights reserved worldwide. www.zondervan.com. The "NIV" and "New International Version" are trademarks registered in the United States Patent and Trademark Office by Biblica, Inc.®

The author is represented by Tom Dean, Literary Agent with A Drop of Ink LLC, www.adropofink.pub.

Regnery books may be purchased in bulk at special discounts for sales promotion, corporate gifts, fund-raising, or educational purposes. Special editions can also be created to specifications. For details, contact the Special Sales Department, Regnery, 307 West 36th Street, 11th Floor, New York, NY 10018 or info@skyhorsepublishing.com.

Regnery® is an imprint of Skyhorse Publishing, Inc.®, a Delaware corporation.

Visit our website at www.regnery.com.
Please follow our publisher Tony Lyons on Instagram @tonylyonsisuncertain.

10 9 8 7 6 5 4 3 2 1

Library of Congress Cataloging-in-Publication Data is available on file.

Cover design by David Ter-Avanesyan
Cover photograph by Molly Taylor

Print ISBN: 978-1-5107-8144-3
eBook ISBN: 978-1-5107-8145-0

Printed in the United States of America

To Mom, Dad, Granny, Paw Paw, Papa Doug, and Nana:

All of you are the reason I am the man I am today. You have been there for me when nobody else was. You have been the best role models I could have ever asked for. You showed me what it is like to live a life in Christ. Your love and support made this book possible, and I can never thank you enough.

This book is dedicated to you.

Don't let anyone look down on you because you are young, but set an example for the believers in speech, in conduct, in love, in faith and in purity.

—1 TIMOTHY 4:12

CONTENTS

CONTENTS

INTRODUCTION

Freedom is a fragile thing and it's never more than **one generation away** *from extinction.*

—*RONALD REAGAN*

It had been eight long years since a Republican had lived in the California governor's mansion. The winds of change were sweeping across the Golden State as a fresh face—a former movie star turned politician—was recently elected to the role of chief executive.

The New Year had kicked off five days ago, and Ronald Wilson Reagan had just delivered a twenty-four-minute address, inspiring hope and promising change. The freshly sworn-in governor delivered a warning that transcended the boundaries of his era:

Freedom is a fragile thing and it's never more than **one generation away** from extinction.[1]

Freedom. What an interesting word. What does it mean to you? What did it mean to Governor Reagan? Why is it fragile—and in America, of all places?

America is often dubbed the "land of the free and the home of the brave." Americans had already beaten those sorry royal loyalists back across the pond in 1776—first with a declaration and then with a revolution rooted in a cry for freedom. America had established itself on the world stage through the innovation of free enterprise and following the Industrial Revolution. Then, in the middle of the twentieth century, America claimed the title of back-to-back world war champs. Surely, freedom was not fragile but was present with an everlasting abundance here in America.

Wrong.

Reagan's words from 1967 force us to reconsider today that freedom isn't something that's conquered once and then kept for eternity; it must be constantly defended. Freedom is a perpetually contested prize.

Yes, freedom is a gift from God, but it is also something that tyrannical overreach can take away.

Filtering the idea of freedom and the words of Ronald Reagan through my Christian worldview, I have come to agree with our fortieth president: Freedom is always at risk of being just one generation away from total extinction.

Why is that?

I learned from a friend who is a licensed counselor that three types of expressions flow out of trouble: *venting, processing*, and *problem-solving*. And what is interesting about these three is that while they are all helpful, the only one that makes progress is problem-solving. Maybe this is why protests seem to go unnoticed by the vast majority of voters. Maybe this is why the Occupy Wall Street movement is all but gone. Maybe our youngest generations today are just like every young generation before us, and all we are doing is venting.

Ronald Reagan never seemed to vent in public. I'm sure he processed a lot of things all the time with trusted advisors and even political adversaries. But I think the reason he is so well remembered is that he was a man of courage, he was funny, he expressed his love for God, and he solved problems. And that is what he did in this speech. Reagan didn't leave us cowering in the darkness after delivering his warning; he gave us the solution as well!

> Freedom is a fragile thing and it's never more than *one generation away* from extinction. It is not ours by way of inheritance; **it must be fought for and defended constantly by each generation,** for it comes only once to a people.[2]

It is fundamentally important for every generation to understand the impact they have on the future of this great experiment called America.

With our everyday freedoms being stripped away, our freedom today is less than one generation away from extinction. If the progressive elites have their way this November, it'll be gone before we know it.

Sometimes History Is Not Worth Repeating

In the line immediately following his famous quote, Reagan warned that "those in world history who have known freedom and then lost it have never known it again."[3]

Consider Germany post-World War I. The Weimar Republic emerged as a beacon of democracy, teeming with transparency and freedom. However, economic turmoil, political unrest, and the ascent of Adolf Hitler's Nazi Party spelled the Republic's downfall in the early 1930s. Once freedoms were eroded, the iron grip of authoritarian rule was established. Germany would not reclaim full democracy until the aftermath of World War II.

Similarly, Russia embarked on a journey toward democracy and political openness following the Soviet Union's dissolution in 1991. But in the early 2000s, Vladimir Putin's leadership ushered in a gradual centralization of power, the complete silencing of opposition, and the suppression of media and basic human rights.

Once freedom is lost, countries go through a great struggle to fully regain it.

Reagan's famous 1967 line is referenced over and over by many who care about the future of our country. But few provide the context of his comment, which I think is even more important and can be used as a guide to help us today. In the line just before this quote, Reagan said, "Perhaps you and I have lived too long with this miracle to properly be appreciative."[4]

Have we grown accustomed to the miracle of freedom? Are we so accustomed to grocery stores always having fresh-baked bread and being able to watch whatever movie we want at any time for only $11.99 a month that we have forgotten the miracle of freedom? Are we spoiled kids demanding everything while appreciating nothing? And I am not talking here about Gen Z. No matter what our parents and grandparents say about us, their parents and grandparents said the very same things about them. (Maybe three things are certain in this world: death, taxes, and complaining about how the next generation is lazy and knows nothing?)

The then fifty-five-year-old California governor was hinting that he expected a future America where the everyday freedoms that his generation—and many generations before—had enjoyed would soon be lost.

The rows of California politicians in the audience and the rest of the state watching through their television screens might have missed it—a quick sentence lodged right between campaign promises and fluffy words about bringing a new day to the state—but the ones that heard it were living in an America so far away from the potential circumstances that the governor foreshadowed that they might have cocked their heads in confusion. At the time, Reagan could have been labeled as a fear-monger, but his message was rooted in a truth that would soon become evident.

Fortunately, Reagan did more than issue a warning; he instilled hope in a nation that had just been dragged through the dumpster fire that was the Jimmy Carter presidency. Some said he could effectively communicate as a result of his previous career as a Hollywood star. Others pointed to his warm, down-to-earth personality that made his fellow Americans feel like he was family. In their eyes, he wasn't a bureaucrat from Washington, DC; he was a familiar friend who had filled their screens for decades. Reagan built a legacy of trust with the American people as an actor before he even considered a run for office. Reagan was just a well-rounded, likable guy, and his impact on not only the Republican Party but the country as a whole is continuing today.

Three and a half decades since leaving office, Ronald Reagan is still polled as the most beloved US president, and I believe it because I can't walk through an airport wearing a "Reagan Bush '84" hat without having dozens of people stop me to tell me how much we need him back in office today. Last year, I was out of the country on a family vacation, thousands of miles from the United States. One day, I threw the hat on while walking out the door and had five people stop me to talk about it on my way to breakfast.

I've been screamed at while walking the streets of our nation's capital for wearing solid red, popularized by another Republican president. But I've never had a negative comment made to me, nor do I feel unsafe or ostracized, when I wear the Gipper's vintage patch hat.

The hat doesn't give me super strength or extra confidence; it simply serves as a reminder of a president who embodied common sense and effectiveness, two things that are greatly missing in Washington, DC, today. While we can't bring Ronald Reagan back, we surely can embrace the ideas he pointed us all toward.

Fourteen years after being sworn in as governor of California, that same movie star turned politician would walk down the steps of the United States Capitol to be sworn in as the fortieth president of the United States. In his 1981 inaugural address, Ronald Reagan echoed the same warning in similar words, but the realization of how close to destruction our values had crept finally was starting to set in.

In his first speech as commander-in-chief, Reagan said, "We're not, as some would have us believe, doomed to an inevitable decline. I do not believe in a fate that will fall on us no matter what we do. I do believe in a fate that will fall on us if we do nothing. So, with all the creative energy at our command, let us begin an era of national renewal. Let us renew our determination, our courage, and our strength. And let us renew our faith and our hope."[5]

Reagan saw the potential threat on the horizon, but he didn't paint a gloomy, doomsday picture. Instead, he reminded Americans of what makes this country great and what we must do to unlock its full potential and set it back on track.

I am not alone in seeing the potential threat on the horizon. The millions of people who voted for the party of Reagan in 2020 are not only aware of the potential threat; some are experiencing tyranny today. And we are standing together doing something about it. This book is my small contribution to the effort.

Not Just an Earthly Battle

When I read Reagan say that he didn't "believe in a fate that will fall on us no matter what we do," but instead one that "will fall on us if we do nothing," I can't help but think of the stories of nations that deviated from God's path and faced the consequences. Countries and cities like Babylon (Jeremiah 51), Sodom (Genesis 18:20), Edom (Jeremiah 49:17–22), and Assyria (Zephaniah 2:13–15) were all prosperous until they started to prioritize their selfishness over following God's divine plan for their lives. Babylon, Sodom, Edom, and Assyria ultimately were all wiped off the face of the planet.

Ronald Reagan warned us in his 1981 inaugural presidential address that if our country doesn't get back on track, the values and way of life that we know and love will be lost forever.

If we had heeded Reagan's first warning on that January morning back in 1967, our country might not be on track to be driven straight into the ground today. But here we are.

Right now in America, many of us are witnessing—and far too many of us are experiencing—brazen violations of our freedoms and fundamental rights before our very eyes. We live in an America that would be unrecognizable to the leaders of our founding era. If you told George Washington, Thomas Jefferson, or Benjamin Franklin that their "shining city on a hill" would one day be arresting political opponents, imposing mandates on their citizens, or blasting propaganda talking points through government-controlled media, they might have turned around and added a few more amendments to the Constitution.

Government overreach went into overdrive in 2020. No, the United States is not on the road to extinction simply because of abuse of power in 2020, but that was the year Americans realized just how much control their government has over them.

What does this control look like?

You're an "anti-democracy fascist threat" if you refuse to get a shot, question election integrity, or don't post a black square to your Instagram feed.

The "fifteen days to slow the spread" of COVID-19 stretched into a three-year-long propaganda campaign, urging—no, demanding—compliance to the government as the ultimate authority. (In all fairness, some of us realized how crazy it all was after a few weeks of quarantine; others are still double-masked while driving in their own car today, but I don't think they are the ones reading this book.)

Parents are having their kids' education and identity stolen from them: Some progressive politicians have openly stated that parents should have no say in their children's curriculum. In the 2021 Virginia governor's race, former governor Terry McAuliffe lost re-election after saying, "I don't think parents should be telling schools what they should teach," in a televised debate.[6] Those ten words ignited suburban parents in Virginian who didn't want a politician blocking all access to their child's public education—where they are required to be five days a week for seven hours a day. That's thirty-five hours a week. A lot of indoctrination can be fit into thirty-five hours if parents are removed from the classroom.

Today, kindergartners are even being brainwashed into believing sex changes are the right thing to do.

How far have we fallen? Kids should be taught their ABCs, not gender-fluid pronouns!

And let's not ignore the fact that advocates of the tax-payer-funded school curriculum are also anti-school choice, so they truly want full control over indoctrinating America's youth with no way for you to get out of it.

Now I know what you're thinking: What does this all have to do with saving American freedom from extinction? Well, like Germany, Russia, and every other country that has bowed its knee to tyranny, America is on the fast track to losing every sense of the values we hold so dear.

> Today, Ronald Reagan's original 1967 warning is more than a prediction; it is reality.

Today, Ronald Reagan's original 1967 warning is more than a prediction; it is reality. In modern-day America, our freedoms and way of life, which have stood the test of time for close to 250 years, are one generation away from total extinction.

A Time for Choosing

This book is not a biography of Ronald Reagan, a historical comparison between America and extinct civilizations, or another debate over COVID-19 lockdowns. Instead, it is a call to embrace our time for choosing. And what a choice we have! Consider Reagan's words to the American people in 1964:

What does it mean whether you hold the deed to the title to your business or property if the government holds the power of life and death over that business or property? And such machinery already exists. The government can find some charge to bring against any concern it chooses to prosecute. Every businessman has his own tale of harassment. Somewhere a perversion has taken place. Our natural, unalienable rights are now considered to be a dispensation of government, and freedom has never been so fragile, so close to slipping from our grasp as it is at this moment.

Our Democratic opponents seem unwilling to debate these issues. They want to make you and I believe that this is a contest between two men, that we're to choose just between two personalities.[7]

Every election has been called "the most important election of our lifetime," but 2024 is different. The stakes could not be higher, and the powers that be in Washington, DC, the globalists, and the Marxists have all gained so much ground in the last one hundred years that America is unrecognizable. They are lying about the history of the United States. They are lying about conservatives. They are lying about racism. They are lying about science. They are lying about climate change. They are lying about embryos. They are lying about elections. They are liars who are unwilling to debate these issues, and they want to make you and me believe that elections are no more than a popularity contest and are never about ideas such as life, liberty, and the pursuit of happiness.

Who are they? Allow me to distinguish *they* from *them*. *They* are the anti-American Marxists who congregate on the very left edge of the Democratic Party. *They* are not Democrats in the tradition of John F. Kennedy, but rather anti-God elitists who are passionately pro-human evolution while being ardently anti-baby. *They* are progressives, meaning that they want America and its values to progress as far away from our founding as quickly as possible, no matter where it goes.

But *they* are not *them*. *Them* are our Democrat colleagues on the other side of the aisle. *Them* are pro-freedom liberals who are part of the Democratic Party for one reason or another. *Them* are your parents and grandparents who have always voted for government support nets, union interests, and the funding of public schools.

I don't have a problem with *them*. I have a problem with the Left, which makes up the *they* who find their home in the Democratic Party.

Throughout the book, I will use *Leftist* and *Marxist* interchangeably, as these are the words commonly used in our political rhetoric today. But please know that I am aiming my concerns squarely at the activists who are leading the charge against America, but I am not including the American voter who votes for Democratic Party candidates.

I promise you this: This book is not full of attacks against low-hanging fruit. It is not a collection of primetime TV zingers or buzzwords strung together to grab headlines. I poured my heart and soul, and most of my junior year of high school, into the research, planning, and writing of this book.

I am a proud Generation Z Christian conservative, and I am writing to my peers and my older brothers and sisters, the Millennials of America. This book is for anybody looking around right now who is concerned about the America their family will grow up in.

Unlike many in my parents' and grandparents' Republican Party, I am no RINO (Republican in Name Only). I am constantly asked why I'm a Republican. Is it because my parents and grandparents are? Is it because I grew up in Alabama? No. While both of those caused me to be raised around conservative ideology, I am a Republican for one simple reason: because I'm a Christian. My faith is my leading beacon in life. I am a Republican because its party platform more closely adheres to conservatism, which is best for all people. I am a conservative because I believe this is the American political ideology that most closely aligns with the teachings of the Bible.

For seven years, I have sat on the sidelines as a commentator encouraging people to vote but not actually being able to do it myself. I am about to vote for the first time in my life this November. I refuse to sit by and watch American freedom corrode. *And I know how—and more importantly why—I'm voting.*

It is time to choose, and if you dare to do so, I invite you to choose freedom just as Ronald Reagan did when he left one party and embraced another because only one party in America has members who proudly—and rightly—proclaim that freedom comes from God.

PART 1
HOW DID WE GET HERE?

CHAPTER 1

The Birth of the American Teenager

*A primary object should be the education of our youth
in the science of government. In a republic, what species
of knowledge can be equally important? And what duty
more pressing than communicating it to those who are
to be the future guardians of the liberties of the country?*
—GEORGE WASHINGTON

The disrespect of the American teenager today is astonishing.

In recent years, the rift between the Boomers and Millennials widened by including such rhetoric as the condescending phrase "Okay, Boomer," and many Boomers and Gen Xers alike began to believe that all Millennials were lazy.

What I find interesting though is the parents of high school students in the 1950s blushed when they saw fan favorite Elvis Presley shake his hips on *The Ed Sullivan Show*. And those same high school students who adored Elvis into the 1960s turned down the radio every time their high school kids turned on classic rock. Then, in the 1990s, when grunge replaced the power ballads of the 1970s and 1980s, another generation of parents rolled their eyes, remembering when music told a story.

Well, I know I am taking it completely out of context, but the Book of Ecclesiastes is right when it says, "there's nothing new under the sun."[1]

My grandparents grew up watching *The Brady Bunch*. My parents grew up watching *Full House*. Imagine for a moment your favorite TV teenager from your favorite classic show. What traits come to mind? Genuine, respectful, polite, understanding, and patient are just a few that pop into my head.

Now, think about what my generation is watching: *Keeping Up With the Kardashians*. Quite the spiral from Greg Brady to D. J. Tanner to Kim K. What happened? What shifted in America that caused our culture to sink so low that our most popular show follows a family who got famous from a sex tape? Are they (and many others like them) the role models we want to put on pedestals for my generation to admire and follow? I don't! But clearly, there are a wicked few in the media and Hollywood who do.

I don't think it's any surprise when I tell you my peers are not the same as the teenagers of the 1960s and 1970s. To understand how we got where we are today, we must first understand how "teenagers" came along in the first place.

The American Teenager

The term "teenager" was coined in the post-WWII Baby Boom when Americans, for the first time, had a gap between childhood and adult responsibilities. According to Google Ngrams, which track the usage of words in literature, the first time the word "teenager" was commonly used was in 1944.[2] From 1944 to the 2010s, the term skyrocketed to the top of the charts as a frequently used word. Little did people know at the time, but this new age group would shape American life forever. With this new phase of life came unprecedented leisure time and the disposable income to enjoy it; it also delayed the embracing of adult responsibilities and even resulted in the absurd notion of "adulting" just a few decades later.

American businesses quickly saw the huge potential in this new market and geared their ads for everything from soda pop to cars to take advantage of kids' growing ability to buy things. Around the same time, companies in the record, radio, TV, and movie industries were also making changes to their products and marketing strategies. Case in point, the music industry quickly turned rock 'n' roll (which in the early 1950s was only played on a few stations but was very popular with the teenagers of the era) into a mass-market phenomenon. This made rock 'n' roll arguably the most popular genre of the twentieth century. And as fear of the out-of-control teenager first emerged, teen rock 'n' roll rebels did not disappoint.

Immediately around the corner from the birth of the American teenager was the war that seemed to go on forever without ever being called a war (it was dubbed "the Vietnam

Conflict," after all). The Vietnam War ushered in America's loss of innocence. It was the age of draft dodging, feminism, and the hippie counterculture, all of which struck a blow to traditional values, and the effects of those eroding values—I believe—is what is causing the confusion and loneliness of American teenagers today.

I'm not alone in understanding the connection. Author and radio talk show host Dennis Prager took on this topic in a five-minute video from PragerU: "Why Are So Many Young People Unhappy?" Acknowledging a Reuters report from 2019 that revealed suicidal thinking, severe depression, and the rate of self-injury among US college students more than doubled in less than ten years,[3] Prager expressed his perspective. While "there are any number of reasons, increased drug and opioid addiction, less human interaction because of cell phone use, and young people's fear for their future are the most widely offered explanations. But the biggest reason is the loss of values and meaning."[4]

A monumental shift occurred in American society after World War II, and this change also affected the lives of teens. In the years after World War II, conservative Christian views had a big impact on the morals and rules of American families, which in turn affected the lives of teenagers. The 1950s and 1960s were a time when conservative Christian values were deeply ingrained in society and helped families and people find their way. In the 1950s, Gallup polls showed that more than 90 percent of adults said they were Christians.[5] Only a small percentage said they were not religious at all or identified with a faith other than Christianity. That's a number almost unimaginable today! For reference, the percentage of adults identifying as Christians today is at 63 percent, as of 2021.[6]

In the same period, nuclear families rooted in traditional Christian ideals were seen as the foundation of a stable and prosperous society, not as taboo. Between 1950 and 1951, 2.5 out of every 1,000 people got divorced. The rate of divorce in 1955 was 2.3 per 1,000. This number was down to 2.1 by 1958.[7] Today, the number of people in America who have been divorced is up all the way to 3.2 per 1,000.[8]

Good societies and the blessings they are to their people always start in the home. And when the "nuclear family" became taboo, America lost its way. Teenagers need a mom and a dad in the home to be raised right. (And a supportive and loving extended family as well as a healthy community helps as well.)

America is failing our youth. Previous generations sat idly by as moral values were thrown out left and right. Today, the prolonged gap between childhood and "adulting" is growing, and it is stunting the maturity and contribution of a whole generation. I'm sure I could point to several scientific sources to justify my point, but allow me to simply say this: I am an American teenager, and all I have to do is look at my peers and compare them to any of the Bradys, and I know that I know that I know. My generation's collective attitudes and behaviors have changed a great deal. They might be more progressive than in the past, but they are by no measure better.

In the years after World War II, conservative Christians stressed how important it was to have strong families, strong religious beliefs, and a sense of community. According to the

National Humanities Center, "Religious membership, church funding, institutional building, and traditional faith and practice all increased in the 1950s. At midcentury, things looked very good for Christian America."[9] Today's American teens, on the other hand, seem to have moved away from these traditional ideals and toward a more secular and individualistic way of thinking. One interesting thing to note is the demise of healthy relationships in the lives of Gen Z, especially when dating.

Conservative Christian values in the middle of the twentieth century stressed purity, abstinence, and the holiness of marriage. Most people held firm to the belief that courtship and marriage were the best ways to find a life partner, and *dating* became the logical means of finding your wife or husband.

Today, there is a clear shift away from these values as more people are more open to casual dating, co-habiting, and putting off getting married until bank accounts and careers have advanced to such a degree that marriage is finally a good idea. According to the Cigna Group, young adults are twice as likely as older adults to be lonely. Seventy-nine percent of people ages eighteen to twenty-four say they feel lonely, but only 41 percent of seniors sixty-six and up say the same thing.[10] (Part of the reason for that may also be because we, as inherently social beings, were locked in our homes for a year and trained to stare at screens instead of faces all day—but we'll get into that more later!) Furthermore, "hook-up culture" has completely ruined the way my generation goes about dating, and it is leaving heartbroken, insecure, frantic kids in its evil wake.

The rise of technology—and most notably social media—has had an enormous impact on my peers: The digital age has made us less likely to talk to each other in person. There is an unending longing for instant gratification created by the way we can now talk to each other instantly, get information in seconds, and see anything we want whenever we want. We have access to everything in the world at our fingertips, and we believe we know everything. And because we have thousands of "friends" online, we feel like we don't need anyone in the real world.

I'd like to take a moment to revisit Ronald Reagan's powerful speech where he talks about American values:

On this day, dedicated to American working men and women, may I tell you the vision I have of a new administration and of a new Congress, filled with new members dedicated to the values we honor today?

But restoring the American dream requires more than restoring a sound, productive economy, vitally important as that is. It requires a return to spiritual and moral values, values so deeply held by those who came here to build a new life. We need to restore those values in our daily life, in our neighborhoods and in our government's dealings with the other nations of the world.

These are the values inspiring those brave workers in Poland. The values that have inspired other dissidents under Communist domination. They remind us that where free unions and collective bargaining are forbidden, freedom is lost. They remind us that freedom is never more than one generation away from

extinction. You and I must protect and preserve freedom here or it will not be passed on to our children.
Today the workers in Poland are showing a new generation not how high is the price of freedom but how
much it is worth that price.[11]

I agree. My generation needs to initiate the necessary change
to return to the moral values that we've lost. Though I've
presented a few major differences between previous generations and my own, and mostly negative ones, I want to make
it clear that I'm not trying to put down my peers. As opposed
to other commentators or authors who go on TV or write
books about the failures of my generation and how we will
never account for anything, I am different because I am a
member of said generation, and I'm here to inspire change.

I am not ashamed to be a member of Generation Z at all.
I might be an "old soul" who reveres the beauty and wisdom
of past generations, but I also admire the passion and potential of my peers. Unlike the doomsday predictors, I see hope
on the horizon if my generation wakes up. I have faith in my
peers. I see our collective capabilities. We have the opportunity to bring about multi-generational change to this great
experiment called *America* and pass on a nation to our kids
and grandkids that is stronger and safer than the one we're
currently being handed. But to do that, we must start now.
The days of sitting on our hands and reposting trendy posts
in support of our favorite causes are over. It's time to speak
out and bring about change before it's too late.

In my introduction, I shared how my generation channels
its frustration. Members of my generation have the opportunity

to decide if they want to vent their frustrations through angry tweets and violent protests or choose to turn their frustrations into a passion to create change. I recently chose to do the latter, and it eventually led to this book you're reading today.

Frustrations Turned into Opportunity, and I Seized It

Some of you have likely noticed a new title next to my name on television: "RNC Youth Advisory Council Co-Chair." This happened because of a hard conversation, or at least what I thought was going to be one.

It was January 2023, and Ronna McDaniel had just been re-elected as chairwoman of the Republican National Committee after a hotly contested campaign. Many in the party argued that they were tired of the recent culture of Republicans losing elections. I was one of those people.

It wasn't just one cycle. Republicans had not won an election cycle since Donald Trump's victory in 2016; Ronna was elected chairwoman in 2017.

I wasn't just a critic of the RNC's recent performance; I endorsed the chairwoman's opponent, Harmeet Dhillon. Harmeet and I met at a conference in Phoenix a few months prior. As one of the best conservative lawyers in the country, it didn't take a lot for her to convince me to support her campaign. I didn't just voice support for Harmeet; I campaigned for her, made calls to RNC committeemen and women, and performed as a surrogate for her on TV.

That's why it was such a shock when I received a text from Ronna's assistant in late January. The chairwoman wanted to set up a call for the next day—Saturday morning. Not only did the newly re-elected chairwoman want to talk, but she was willing to commit her Saturday morning to do it. I didn't know what to make of her request, since I had never met Ronna. Was this a call to rub her win in my face? Was this her notice to me that I would be blacklisted from the party for going against the "establishment"? I didn't know what to expect.

I texted back with my first available meeting time for the next morning. Her team accepted. The call was set.

I immediately started phoning friends. The first one was to a former employee of the RNC. She had served as a state party chairwoman for years and knew Ronna well. My next call was to my state's newly inaugurated US senator, Katie Britt. (I had just flown home from her swearing-in ceremony a few days prior.) Senator Britt was serving on the RNC's 2024 election advisory council alongside some of the party's top-name candidates from the 2022 midterms. I asked them both how to handle the call. They both said to be confident, but that's easier said than done. Telling the leader of the party what I thought she was doing wrong would not be easy, but it was necessary.

Early Saturday morning, I finished my earlier meetings and prepared for my call with the chairwoman. I wrote three notes on a small piece of paper in shorthand:

1. Youth Council w/ actual input
2. Open line of communication
3. Win!!!

It started with the pleasantries, which I always entertain for the first five minutes, and then I got to business. "Madam

Chairwoman," I said, "I think it's past time the party forms a youth advisory council. The DNC formed theirs in 2003. We are almost twenty years behind them, and Generation Z and Millennials will make up nearly half of American voters in 2024."

The line was silent. I took a deep breath, letting it sink in that I had just pitched an idea to the chairwoman within just a few minutes of meeting her after spending months campaigning against her. What was her reaction going to be? I had no idea.

"I love it," she replied. "Let's do it."

Wow. That was easy!

I responded with, "Awesome, but I just want to confirm that this won't be for looks. This will be an actual operating fast track to give input to the RNC so we can win the election next year. And when something's going wrong, I don't want to have to go through a team of assistants to voice my concerns. I want an open line of communication so we can be transparent."

Ronna replied, "Of course. Done. I'll give you my cell number."

Then it was her turn to talk. She said this was the reason she set up the call. Although I was on television speaking against her, she liked the ideas I was presenting. She acknowledged that the GOP had not succeeded in past efforts to connect with young voters and that connecting with my generation would be one of the top priorities of her new term as chair. She was calling to see what ideas I had for youth engagement, but before she had the chance to ask, I had already made my pitch.

Then she asked something that would alter the course of the next two years of my life. "If I form this council, will you chair it?"

Wow. I went into this call fearing I was about to be black-listed from the national party, and now I'm being asked to chair a new council!

"Of course, but I can't do this by myself."

"That's OK," she said. "Pick a co-chair, draft a list of members, and send it to us, and we'll get back to you."

And that was that! I hung up the phone and called CJ Pearson.

When I first entered the political arena in 2017, there was one other vocal young conservative on all of social media: CJ. We became fast friends and grew even closer when he decided to go to college at the University of Alabama.

By this time, CJ had left UA to move to Los Angeles to work for PragerU. It had only been a few weeks, and we were still unpacking. (Funny story: He got locked out of his new apartment while I was pitching him the idea of a co-chair position over the phone. After finding his landlord to let him in, CJ accepted my offer.)

We enthusiastically compiled a draft list of potential members, and soon, the Republican National Committee formed its inaugural Youth Advisory Council. After nearly twenty years of being behind the leaps and bounds of the DNC, the RNC was quickly making future-altering prog-ress. Why? Because of hard conversations.

My favorite inspirational quote is, "Don't wait for oppor-tunity. Create it." That quote has been the mantra of my life. I saw our party was failing with youth engagement. I didn't wait for a youth advisory council to be founded; I called the chairwoman and pitched the idea myself. That needs to be the mantra of my generation. Bring about change through effective determination, not senseless screaming and rant posts.

> *Bring about change through effective determination, not senseless screaming and rant posts.*

I don't tell that story to toot my own horn or highlight my negotiating skills. I share it to explain the power of presenting new, out-of-the-box thinking and the need to have the courage to be willing to put those ideas into action. The Republican Party has a reputation for being old and slow, especially when considering party platforms and policies; I've often referred to the Grand Old Party as a slow-moving freight train trying to drive through tar. And maybe this has contributed to why we haven't won an election cycle since 2016. But right now, it seems we are moving in the right direction, at least with the younger generations who are the future of America.

CHAPTER 2

The Marxists Get to Work

Political language . . . is designed to make lies sound truthful and murder respectable, and to give an appearance of solidity to pure wind.

—GEORGE ORWELL

I had just wrapped up a twenty-nine-page speech about the need for youth engagement in modern-day politics.

My audience? Mostly Boomers attending their local Republican Party meeting. I urged them to talk to their kids and grandkids about making plans to vote in the upcoming election and to be open to electing a new generation into office. I fielded thirty minutes of questions after the speech about issues ranging from election integrity to how good of a handshake Donald Trump has. After answering their questions, I stepped away from the podium.

A lady stopped me as I was making my way off the stage with a frightened look on her face.

"I'm sorry," she said.

"For what?" I asked.

"For leaving you with a country like this," she said.

I stood there for a second, thinking about how to appropriately respond. "Ma'am, this isn't your fault. You've just left us with a challenge, but we're going to turn this country around, don't you worry."

She stopped me again and said, "No, it was those dang hippie professors. We should have stopped it when they first came in."

A few weeks later, I sat down to write out the table of contents for this book. I took out a yellow legal pad and jotted down a bird's eye skeleton of what I wanted this book to cover. A few days later, I showed it to a friend.

"Teachers?" he said. "You're starting your book talking about teachers?"

"Yes."

"OK. Whatever. But you can't label them as Marxists."

"Of course I can, because the ones who infiltrated higher education had one goal: to spread their communist agenda into the minds of our youngest, most vulnerable citizens."

So yes, I am addressing early on in this book what I believe is the main reason my generation is brainwashed today—public school educators—and I won't be holding any punches because they didn't!

Understanding the "Isms"

Before we get to the activists, I mean "educators," let's back it up and talk about the agenda they're spreading. And to do so, we need a simple starting point on the differences between Marxism, communism, and socialism.

Marxism

Marxism is an ideology. It is a philosophy on life offered by Karl Marx (hence Marx-ism). Karl Marx wrote *The Communist Manifesto*, the original guide for self-identifying communists to carry out their Marxist ideas.

> Oxford Dictionary: the political and economic theories of Karl Marx (1818–83) which explain the changes and developments in society as the result of opposition between the social classes.[1]

Communism

Communism is a form of government. It is commonly installed to put into practice the ideology of Marxism and is marked by central planning, a large bureaucracy dedicated to the "common good," and single-party rule.

> Oxford Dictionary: A theory or system of social organization in which all property is owned by the community and each person contributes and receives according to their ability and needs.[2]

Socialism

Socialism is an economic theory. Often connected to Marxism's idea of class warfare, socialism is concerned with the quality of life for the working class, high taxes on the middle and upper classes, strong regulations, and public ownership of services for "the common good."

> Oxford Dictionary: A set of political and economic theories based on the belief that everyone has an equal right to a share of a country's wealth and that the government should own and control the main industries.[3]

OK, now that we have common ground in understanding these seemingly interchangeable words, what do they look like in action? I think Saul Alinsky's *Rules for Radicals: A Pragmatic Primer for Realistic Radicals* offers the most tangible expression of how Marxism shows up in every facet of America today. His rules for creating change are:

1. Power is not only what you have, but what the enemy thinks you have.
2. Never go outside the experience of your people.
3. Whenever possible go outside the experience of your enemy.
4. Make your enemy live up to their own book of rules.
5. Ridicule is man's most potent weapon.
6. A good tactic is one your people enjoy.
7. A tactic that drags on too long becomes a drag.
8. Keep the pressure on.

9. The threat is usually more terrifying than the threat itself.
10. The major premise for tactics is the development of operations that will maintain constant pressure upon the opposition.
11. If you push a negative hard and deep enough it will break through to its counter-side.
12. The price of a successful attack is a constructive alternative.
13. Pick the target, freeze it, personalize it, and polarize it.[4]

And what do Marxists want to change? They want to reinvent the faith of our Founding Fathers. They want to change American history. They want to prove America is responsible for all the world's problems, even those that existed before 1619—the year the first slaves were brought to our shores. They want to ignore the rule of law. They want to eradicate Christian charity from the world and replace it with government handouts. They want to live in a world free from belief in heaven and hell and the consequences of sin. They want to live in a world where a man can be a woman, a girl can be a cat, and the sky is falling. Vladimir Lenin was open about this. He said the quiet part out loud and revealed the end game when he said, "the goal of socialism is communism."[5] He was a man who knew a lot about both, so his remark should not be ignored.

So what does Marxism really look like?

Sexual revolutionists love to wield Rule 4 as they decry the "hypocrisy" of the Church.

The media gleefully enacts Rule 5, ridiculing anyone and everyone who loves faith, family, or freedom.

Marxists love to abuse "climate change" as a tactic for Rule 9 because they know and understand Rule 7. What was once "global cooling" became "global warming" and is now whatever they want it to be.

Big government is the operation the Left has built to deploy Rule 10.

Evolutionists fear the argument of "an intelligent designer" because intelligent Christians are using Rule 12 against them.

And, if we learn nothing else from the response of governments around the world to the COVID-19 pandemic, it is that Rule 13 reigns supreme. Because polarization leads to fear, and fear leads to those in charge being given more and more power.

Explaining "Cultural Marxism," Jeff Myers, president of Summit Ministries,[6] says, "The writings of Marx, Marx's co-author Friedrich Engels, and later writings by V.I. Lenin and Mao Zedong run into the hundreds of volumes. But it is crystal clear in all these writings that institutions such as the economic system, the government, religion, and family are inherently oppressive."[7]

So to any parents reading this now, if your kids' "educators" believe that your ability to work to buy groceries, the country you love, your faith, and even your home are "inherently oppressive," why would you ever let your kid be a student of their worldview? I've heard it said on conservative radio talk shows that the problem with college today is that kids come home at Thanksgiving having learned it is right for them to hate their parents. That can't be true. Could it?

The Seeds of Communism

A communist revolution, in which communism rules over the whole world, has always been the Marxists' end goal. It was Vladimir Lenin, the Russian revolutionary and politician, who first put Marx's ideas into practice with the power of a government; he was the founder of the Soviet Union.

In his book *The State and Revolution*, Lenin identifies the influence of Marx on his political ideology and plans, saying that his "first task is to restore the true doctrine of Marx on the State."[8] His goal was a world revolution in favor of the elites at the expense of the middle class by wielding the poor and the workers as his weapons. And he never tried to hide it, since he also said, "As an ultimate goal, 'peace' just means communist control of the whole world."[9]

In communists' worldview, there is no room for God. There is no room for Jesus, the true bringer of peace: "Peace I leave with you; my peace I give you. I do not give to you as the world gives. Do not let your hearts be troubled and do not be afraid" (John 14:27). There is only "heaven on earth" without God.

Communists—and their friends (because the enemy of my enemy is my friend)—want every good thing from God and Christianity without having to bother with Jesus and the Church. They want personal identity without a Creator, love without commitment, community without fellowship, faith without God, and hope without heaven. And they are doing everything they can to eradicate God from the public square.

The anti-God, pro-power elites have sought to gain more and more control around the world so that one day, the whole world will give in to communism. To reach their main goal of communist world rule, the communists sought to infiltrate groups and forces that were against communism, including the Catholic Church and the United States government. Their goal was to turn these enemies into allies from the inside.

When the communists planned their attack, they were very organized, careful, and patient. They knew that to change the policy and way of thinking of a whole country, like the United States, from being against communism to supporting it, they would have to change the way its people thought. So they would have to go after kids and teens, from toddlers to young adults, and shape their thoughts in a way that supports socialism, communism, and Marxism. People say that Lenin said, "Give me four years to teach the children, and the seed I have sown shall never be uprooted." To do that, they invaded America by planting roots in our schools and universities.

The Sprouts We're Seeing Today

Let me preface this by saying that my mom was a teacher. Both of my grandmothers were educators. In kindergarten, I wanted to be a teacher! Imagine that! (That dream quickly faded, and four years later I somehow entered politics.) My point is that I have tremendous respect for teachers. I fully understand that not all teachers are Marxists; in fact, most of them aren't, but there are a growing number of liberal activists mixed in the bunch that are enough to indoctrinate a generation and give the entire profession a bad reputation. When activists infiltrated education, that's when everything went wrong.

First, it was higher education. From 1969 to 1998, 40 to 45 percent of faculty in America's universities were made up of self-identified liberals.[10] In 1998, professors who identified as conservatives made up 18 percent of American colleges' faculty. In 2013, it was

> *When activists infiltrated education, that's when everything went wrong.*

as low as 12 percent.[11] Most of our schools and universities have slowly changed from places that encourage free speech to incubators for cultural Marxism to grow.

Don't believe me? Consider this: Harvard, perhaps the pinnacle of education in the United States, started as a theological seminary. According to the Christian Heritage Fellowship, "Only eighteen years after the Pilgrims landed in the New World, Harvard College, the first of the Ivy League schools, was established for the sake of educating the clergy and raising a Christian academic institution to meet the needs of perpetuating the Christian faith. All of the Ivy League schools were established by Christians for the sake of advancing Christianity and meeting the academic needs of the New World."[12]

So what happened? How did all of the Ivy League schools go from teaching the Bible to teaching "everything in the world is good, except the Bible"?

In short, it is the anti-God movement popularized by Karl Marx and his sidekick Friedrich Engels. According to historian and professor Benjamin Wiker,

> Both Marx and Engels were atheists, and atheists don't like bothersome spiritual things. Therefore, they

disallow them from existing and count on everything being purely material. That makes things very simple. Simplicity of a sort can be a kind of virtue. But the simplicity of Marxist reductionist materialism is a dreadful vice precisely because it ignores the complexity of the very things it professes to explain: human beings and human history.[13]

Most atheists who adopt the ideas of Marx and Engels and put into practice Alinsky's rules do so because they don't like God, they hate Christians, and they despise Jews. We have seen it in the Soviet Union under Lenin. We fought against it in Germany when we went to war against the Nazis. We have protected the nation of Israel from it today in the Middle East. And now, the once God-fearing and neighbor-loving students at Harvard are holding anti-Israel and pro-Hamas rallies on college campuses and calling for the genocide of the Jews with the support of their leadership![14] And thanks to Congresswoman Elise Stefanik of New York, we have the sick hatred and perverted ideology of Marxism in the congressional record.

On December 5, 2023, Congresswoman Stefanik questioned then-Harvard President Claudine Gay about ongoing anti-Semitic and anti-Israel bigotry on the Harvard campus following the Hamas terrorist attack on October 7, 2023. Here is the Hollywood-worthy transcript. Read it like you are watching a movie. Be entertained and frightened by the quick dialogue. It is lengthy, but it is necessary because it reveals the battle that we are in. It shows how the anti-God Marxist ideology of the Left has infiltrated the American education system. It shows how the Left lies. And, thanks to Congresswoman Stefanik, it shows what it looks like to defend freedom.

> **Congresswoman Stefanik:** Dr. Gay, a Harvard student calling for the mass murder of African Americans is not protected free speech at Harvard, correct?
>
> **President Gay:** Our commitment to free speech—
>
> **Congresswoman Stefanik:** It's a yes or no question. Is that correct? Is that okay for students to call for the mass murder of African Americans at Harvard? Is the protected free speech?
>
> **President Gay:** Our commitment to free speech—
>
> **Congresswoman Stefanik:** It's a yes or no question. Let me ask you this: you are president of Harvard so I assume you are familiar with the term "Intifada," correct?
>
> **President Gay:** I have heard that term, yes.
>
> **Congresswoman Stefanik:** And you understand that the use of the term "intifada" in the context of the Israeli-Arab conflict is indeed a call for violent armed resistance against the State of Israel, including violence against civilians and the genocide of Jews. Are you aware of that?
>
> **President Gay:** That type of hateful speech is personally abhorrent to me.
>
> **Congresswoman Stefanik:** And there have been multiple marches at Harvard with students chanting "There is only one solution. Intifada revolution" and "Globalize the Intifada," is that correct?

President Gay: I've heard that thoughtless, reckless, and hateful language on our campus, yes.

Congresswoman Stefanik: So based upon your testimony, you understand that this call for intifada is to commit genocide against the Jewish people in Israel and globally, correct?

President Gay: I will say again, that type of hateful speech is personally abhorrent to me.

Congresswoman Stefanik: Do you believe that type of hateful speech is contrary to Harvard's Code of Conduct or is it allowed at Harvard?

President Gay: It is at odds with the values of Harvard.

Congresswoman Stefanik: Can you not say here that it is against the Code of Conduct at Harvard?

President Gay: We embrace a commitment to free expression even of views that are objectionable, offensive, hateful—it's when that speech crosses into conduct that violates our policies against bullying, harassment, intimidation . . .

Congresswoman Stefanik: Does that speech not cross that barrier? Does that speech not call for the genocide of Jews and the elimination of Israel? You testified that you understand that that is the definition of "intifada." Is that speech according to the Code of Conduct or not?

President Gay: We embrace a commitment to free expression and give a wide berth to free expression even of views that are objectionable, outrageous, and offensive.

Congresswoman Stefanik: You and I both know that that is not the case. You are aware that Harvard ranked dead last when it came to free speech, are you not aware of that report?

President Gay: As I've observed earlier, I reject that characterization of our campus.

Congresswoman Stefanik: The data show it's true and isn't it true that Harvard previously rescinded multiple offers of admission for applicants and accepted freshmen for sharing offensive memes, and racist statements, sometimes as young as sixteen years old. Did Harvard not rescind those offers of admission?

President Gay: That long predates my time as president so I can't speak.

Congresswoman Stefanik: But you understand that Harvard made that decision to rescind those offers of admission.

President Gay: I have no reason to contradict the facts as you present them to me.

Congresswoman Stefanik: Correct, because it's a fact. You're also aware that a Winthrop House faculty dean was let go over who he chose to legally represent. Correct? That was while you were dean.

President Gay: That is an incorrect characterization of what transpired.

Congresswoman Stefanik: What's the characterization?

President Gay: I'm not going to get into details about a personnel matter.

Congresswoman Stefanik: Well let me ask you this: Will admission offers be rescinded or any disciplinary action taken against students or applicants who say, "from the river to the sea" or "intifada" advocating for the murder of Jews?

President Gay: As I've said, that type of hateful, reckless, offensive speech is personally abhorrent to me.

Congresswoman Stefanik: No action will be taken? What action will be taken?

President Gay: When speech crosses into conduct that violates our policies, including policies against bullying, harassment, and intimidation, we take action. We have robust disciplinary processes that allow us to hold individuals accountable.

Congresswoman Stefanik: What action has been taken against students who are harassing and calling for the genocide of Jews on Harvard's campus?

President Gay: I can assure you that we have robust disciplinary actions.

Congresswoman Stefanik: What actions have been taken? I'm not asking, I'm asking what actions have been taken against those students.

President Gay: Given students' rights to privacy and our obligations under FERPA. I will not say more about any specific cases other than to reiterate that processes are ongoing.

Congresswoman Stefanik: Do you know what the number one hate crime in America is?

President Gay: I know that over the last couple of months, there has been an alarming rise of antisemitism which I understand is the critical topic that we are here to discuss.

Congresswoman Stefanik: That's correct. It is anti-Jewish hate crimes. And Harvard ranks the lowest when it comes to protecting Jewish students. This is why I have called for your resignation and your testimony today and not being able to answer with moral clarity speaks volumes.[15]

The seeds sown by Marxists in our education system decades ago are sprouting today as anti-Semitism is running rampant in our education systems. And there is nothing closer to anti-God thinking than anti-Semitism.

Had the protests had anything to do with decrying the agendas of the LGBTQ+ activists, pro-choice activists, BLM, or even against Critical Race Theory, the student involved would have been wholly condemned by the leadership at Harvard. But because it was an attack on the Jews, the anti-God Marxists applauded it and when called out for it, they attempted to hide behind rhetoric.

One hundred years ago, such a congressional hearing would have gone like this:

Congresswoman: Do you believe that this type of hateful speech, calling for the genocide of a single group of people, in this case Jews, is contrary to Harvard's Code of Conduct, or is it allowed at Harvard?

President: It is at odds with the values of Harvard. It is contrary to Harvard's Code of Conduct. It is contrary to the teachings of the Bible. There is no place for it at Harvard or in any corner of America. The students have been reprimanded. And the administrators, faculty, and students of Harvard would like to publicly apologize to the students on our campus who have been threatened and made to feel unsafe, to their parents who have entrusted their children to us, to the Jewish community with whom we stand, and to Americans as a whole. We are sorry. This will never happen again at Harvard.

This takeover of the American education system was orchestrated. This was a planned operation to turn America's youth into brainwashed activists of the Radical Left. Today, we're seeing the tentacles of this operation all the way down to elementary schools. But it's not just education. Liberal propaganda has infiltrated media, sports, government offices, and even the private sector. Anywhere you have malcontents, look for communists around them.

One of the problems I have with recent language is Millennials and Gen Z have basically been labeled as malcontents. I often wonder, is that true, and why? To whatever extent it is true, it's because we're not being taught what evil is. Dennis Prager said this about what evil looks like in our society:

Most of our schools teach almost nothing of importance, and nothing is more important than the study of good and evil. In the United States today, nearly all schools, from elementary through graduate, concentrate on teaching about racism, sexism, preferred pronouns, homophobia, transphobia, LGBTQIA+, climate change, diversity, equity, inclusiveness and white guilt. In other words, most of our educational institutions, including the most prestigious, do not educate.[16]

He's exactly right. Our public education system has turned in to a propaganda machine for the approved, progressive narrative. Unfortunately, the orchestration doesn't stop in the classrooms.

When people got upset and went to the streets over inequalities in America in 2020 during the George Floyd protests, you better believe modern-day communists sprung on that opportunity to stroke the flames and were out there with them. During protests by feminists and the LGBTQ crowd, we saw Marxist ideology as well as Antifa find their way in to take advantage of the rallies to advance their anti-law defund the police agenda. Today, people look around and wonder how communists even got into *Sesame Street*, Disney, and the NFL. That's when you have to remind yourself that this was a well-organized, coordinated attack on every aspect of American life, including what we watch, and most importantly, let our children watch.

A lot of what we see in businesses and institutions today comes from Marxist ideas. They didn't take over all of Big Business right away. They did not start in the boardrooms; they started in Human Resources, where they encouraged class warfare inside the organization. The company would slowly become more Marxist and less capitalist, more progressive and less conservative, more secular and less religious, more global and less American. They did it on purpose as they are determined to destroy the Western way of life because freedom terrifies them.

It was not that long ago that Americans cheered when their president Ronald Reagan went to West Berlin, Germany, and challenged then leader of the Soviet Union Mikhail Gorbachev to choose for his people between the blessing of a free society and the burden of communist socialism, saying,

> We welcome change and openness; for we believe that freedom and security go together, that the advance of human liberty can only strengthen the cause of world peace. There is one sign the Soviets can make that would be unmistakable, that would advance dramatically the cause of freedom and peace. General Secretary Gorbachev, if you seek peace, if you seek prosperity for the Soviet Union and eastern Europe, if you seek liberalization, come here to this gate. Mr. Gorbachev, open this gate. Mr. Gorbachev, tear down this wall.[17]

Reagan was drawing the world's attention to the oppression that came from Marxist ideology—in this case, in the form of the communist government of the Soviet Union, whose socialist economic policies resulted in the construction of the Berlin Wall. The wall? I'm glad you asked. It was a concrete barrier with guard towers that surrounded East Berlin to prevent the East German citizens who lived there from fleeing the dismal life they lived under the control of the communist government in favor of the freedom and prosperity provided by the countries of "Western civilization."

While Americans might have cheered when word of President Reagan's conviction and courage made it across the pond, the people of East Berlin surely celebrated their new-found freedom when, in 1990, the political leaders of Eastern Europe did exactly what the "leader of the free world" challenged then to do: they tore down the wall.

So if we American teens want to be taken seriously, we have to take ourselves seriously, we have to take ideas seriously, and we really should figure out which ideas are the best. Shouldn't we?

In the introduction, I mentioned Ronald Reagan's famous "A Time for Choosing" speech (my all-time favorite speech in history!), in which he argued that "they want to make you and I believe that this is a contest between two men—that we're to choose just between two personalities."[18] Well, it's not. It's a battle of ideas, and the personalities are just part of the messenger.

What the world needs is a message of truth. I love that President Reagan pointed to truth often, and he was bold in doing so. Perhaps his most profound commentary on the world we live in was his remarks at the Annual Convention of the National Association of Evangelicals:

> There is sin and evil in the world, and we're enjoined by Scripture and the Lord Jesus to oppose it with all our might. Our nation, too, has a legacy of evil with which it must deal. The glory of this land has been its capacity for transcending the moral evils of our past. For example, the long struggle of minority citizens for equal rights, once a source of disunity and civil war, is now a point of pride for all Americans. We must never go back. There is no room for racism, anti-Semitism, or other forms of ethnic and racial hatred in this country.

I know that you've been horrified, as have I, by the resurgence of some hate groups preaching bigotry and prejudice. Use the mighty voice of your pulpits and the powerful standing of your churches to denounce and isolate these hate groups in our midst. The commandment given us is clear and simple: "Thou shalt love thy neighbor as thyself."

But whatever sad episodes exist in our past, any objective observer must hold a positive view of American history, a history that has been the story of hopes fulfilled and dreams made into reality. Especially in this century, America has kept alight the torch of freedom, but not just for ourselves but for millions of others around the world.[19]

CHAPTER 3

Hello, Hippies . . . Goodbye, Morals

If you do not take an interest in the affairs of your government, then you are doomed to live under the rule of fools.

—PLATO

What I appreciate from some of the quality television shows in recent years is that they rip their storylines from the headlines.

Writer Aaron Sorkin is renowned for such a strategy in both his television series *The West Wing* and *The Newsroom*, which examine the lives and ideologies of government employees and media personalities, respectively. In one episode of *The Newsroom*, Sorkin displays the tension that exists between the inept ideology of Marxism when applied in the real world and the pragmatism of capitalism when coupled with a free society.

Let me set the stage for you. A nightly news show featuring on-air talent Will McAvoy is interviewing a woman who is part of the Occupy Wall Street movement. McAvoy is a fifty-plus-year-old, white, moderate Republican (but hardly a conservative). Shelly Wexler is a mid-twenties schoolteacher and part-time activist. Here's the scene:

> **Will:** It's been two weeks since a group of protesters began camping out in Zucotti Park here in New York City. The Occupy Wall Street movement has turned to social media and held marches through the streets of the financial district. Here in the studio today is one of the leaders of Occupy Wall Street, Shelly Wexler. Shelly, thanks for being with us.
> **Shelly:** It's good to be here, but I am not one of the leaders of OWS. We don't have leaders.
> **Will:** Is that a good idea?
> **Shelly:** Not having leaders?
> **Will:** Yeah.
> **Shelly:** Yes, because this way, everyone's sure to have a voice.
> **Will:** Sounds like a lot of people talking at once. But tell us in a few words what OWS is protesting.
> **Shelly:** We are protesting a variety of issues, the co-opting of the government by the rich, the lack of any prosecution for the crimes that led to the collapse of 2008, Citizens United, social inequality.

Will: So not any particular thing?

Shelly: Not one particular thing.

Will: You're protesting against lots of things?

Shelly: The list of things we're protesting against is as varied as the protesters themselves.

Will: I've seen protesters holding signs that say, "We are the 99%."

Shelly: Yes.

Will: I am the 1%. Some people would say I'm over-paid, but I'm not. I'm paid exactly what the market will bear, which means I'm paid what I'm worth. So which system would you replace capitalism with?

Shelly: We wouldn't . . . I wouldn't replace it with any system. I would make the system fairer.

Will: By passing new laws?

Shelly: Yes.

Will: It's Congress who does that.

Shelly: Yes.

Will: It's legislation like Dodd-Frank that the banks really fear, right?

Shelly: Yes.

Will: If your congressman or your senator or the Chairman of the House Financial Services Committee or the Speaker of the House wanted to hear the demands of OWS, who would they meet with?

Shelly: We're not looking for a meeting.

Will: They wouldn't be able to meet with anyone, right?

Shelly: Look . . .

Will: I'm trying to find the virtue of a leaderless movement where everyone's voices are heard.

Shelly: That isn't the point. We want everyone to look at Occupy Wall Street and ask themselves the question, "Why is this happening?"

Will: I think that's been taken care of. But what happens after people ask themselves that?

Shelly: Change, we hope.

Will: How?

Shelly: The same way change has always happened.

Will: What is your best-case scenario for how this ends?

Shelly: That it doesn't end.

Will: That it doesn't end?

Shelly: That's right.

Will: Even if you put the heads of the banks in jail, overturn a Supreme Court decision, ensure greater social equality and give everybody money, you're still going to be sleeping in Zucotti Park?

Shelly: Like most of the media, I don't think you're taking this seriously.

Will: Is there any chance that's because you're not?[1]

If the American teen wants to be taken seriously, we need to take ourselves and our values, as well as our families and country, seriously. We need to start paying attention to the world we live in and not the pretend world of Instagram and TikTok. And we need to take the threat of Marxist ideology seriously, and maybe put the phone down and play outside more.

Let's pick up the conversation between Will and Shelly. A lot has happened, and believe it or not, the almost "Boomer" is sorry for how he embarrassed Shelly on national TV. Meeting with her in the hallway outside of her classroom, they continue their dance before coming to a sincere apology and a moment of learning for both of them:

Shelly: I can't believe what it takes to get you to apologize.
Will: I have absolutely no intention of apologizing. But you should enjoy me while I'm here, 'cause as soon as I leave, so does the attention. Your movement sucks, Shelly.
Shelly: I'm sure it looks that way from the outside.
Will: And right there is your problem, 'cause who the **** cares what it looks like from the inside? Slavery, suffrage, civil rights, Vietnam, what all those things have in common is there were leaders. And the only thing the leaders cared about was getting it done. And if you guys had leaders who could find a map with a ****'n map, they'd tell you the thing about capitalism is it's politically accountable. Did you watch my show tonight? Did you see anybody courting the OWS vote? 'Cause all eight candidates for the Republican nomination said the words "Tea Party" today in a bite they knew would get picked up.
Shelly: We're not trying to get anyone elected. We're just trying to point so that people will look. And you're looking at us and not what we're pointing at.[2]

Wow. In just a few words, we get a survey of American history: slavery, the right to vote, civil rights, Vietnam, leadership, capitalism, accountability, geography, politics, Occupy Wall Street protests, and the Tea Party. But what we also get is that the one of the keys to being taken seriously is to point to something more meaningful than ourselves. That is a lesson that both my generation of future leaders and the GOP at large need to understand.

The key to choosing today, in our modern era of soundbites and headlines, is not to look at the messenger but at the message they are pointing to. We can't look at a political candidate today and vote for them based on their eloquence, humor, or intellect. We probably shouldn't even vote for them based on their ideas. We should vote based on the ideas of those they point to.

Me? I point to Ronald Reagan because he pointed to the Founding Fathers, and they pointed to our "Creator."

What or whom are the Marxists, communists, socialists, environmentalists, globalists, and all of the social justice activists pointing to? Because it is definitely not the wisdom of the American Founders or the capital "G" God they all revere.

This Is Not New

America has a long history of protests, from the Boston Tea Party and Women's suffrage movement to the civil rights marches and the Vietnam War sit-ins, and more recently, the Occupy Wall Street movement and BLM protests. My question is, are we just venting our considerable disappointments in life and in government? Are we at least processing the ideas being presented to us in a sincere effort to discover right and wrong? Or are we adding to the public discourse in an effort to solve real problems faced by Americans? I suggest that it may be a combination of all three, but more recently, there has been a whole lot of venting without any real problem-solving.

The idea of traditional morality became a relic of the past when, in the 1960s, young people tuned in, turned on, and tuned out. Their mantra never to trust anyone over the age of thirty was solidified when the Watergate scandal made the entire country more cynical and distrustful of American institutions.

But the concerns of the time should have been less about what culture of life hippies were perpetuating and instead about the titanic shift it would have on the political land-scape for decades—if not centuries—to come.

It seems to me something changed between the black and white television shows of the 1950s and 1960s and the gang-ster rap of the 1980s and 1990s. I don't believe I'm alone in my thinking. All one has to do is watch movies from 1960s and 1970s and see plainly that a lax attitude has prevailed, and topics that were once off the table became topics at the dinner table. And it led to awkward conversations twenty years later when Americans who had grown up and were taught not to say the word "pregnant" in polite company were now parents having to explain to their children the stain on a White House intern's blue dress. Mark Twain once said, "Man is the only animal that blushes. Or needs to."[3] America has forgotten how to blush.

Everybody loves to focus on what the hippies got wrong, but before we get into that, let's ask the question: What did they get right? They realized that the US government was corrupt. They realized institutions of higher learning were beginning to think too highly of themselves. Most importantly, they learned not to trust figures of political power.

The movement also brought the reminder that protests were able to change people's minds. That's why the first right laid out in the Bill of Rights is "the right to assemble." In the past, Americans had faith in the choices made by the military-industrial complex and went to war when their numbers were called. In 1967 and 1968, protests on college campuses grew and turned into groups that led to the campaigns of Robert F. Kennedy and Eugene McCarthy. America was founded on protests. If our Founding Fathers had sat by idly as they were frustrated with the way things were, then we would not be a country today. Good, genuine, thoughtful protests can be effective, and this era reminded Americans of that.

As for downsides, the hippie movement in America brought more polarization to a country everyone thought couldn't get more polarized (if only they could see us today!). The Baby Boomer generation started to split into two groups with very different views when Reserve Officers Training Corps (ROTC) programs and new hippies started to argue with each other on college campuses.

And the normalization of "recreational drug use" drove a huge stake in the heart of American morals and started the current era of our streets being crowded with homeless people addicted to drugs.

But nobody thought that far ahead at the time. The hippies were about what felt good at the time, with no concern for how degrading it could be in the future, which leads me to my next point. The hippie era brought about short-term living which led to a culture of selfishness. This also led to a world where people stopped caring about their neighbors and only cared about themselves.

> *The hippie era brought about short-term living which led to a culture of selfishness.*

What was good for you at the moment was the right decision. It was tempting to only think about the present moment after the "Summer of Love." There was a general lack of hope for the future because of the Vietnam War, Watergate, and the assassinations of 1968. It was hard to plan and think about the future because people felt like they were nearing the end. The mindset of the time was a far cry from "Live Free or Die." The thinking at the time might have been more of a "Live Free and Die" mindset.

A Time of Decaying Principles

In his 1967 inaugural gubernatorial address, Ronald Reagan talked about the moral deterioration of America. He said, "The deterioration of every government begins with the decay of the principle upon which it was founded. This was written in 1748, and it's as true today as it was then. Government is the people's business, and every man, woman and child becomes a shareholder with the first penny of tax paid."[4]

Keep in mind, the quote he shared was said in 1748, and the year he included it in his speech was 1967, but per usual, the Gipper accurately predicted the lasting effects of the decay of morals. Little did he know, just a few decades later, morals would go out the window entirely, and any talks of high standards would be taboo.

I didn't live through the hippie revolution, but I am living through a modern-day rebellion, and as a teenager, I think I have an interesting perspective.

Why did this all begin? Teenagers in the 1960s wanted "freedom." They wanted to be able to do what they wanted and not suffer the consequences. They wanted freedom from everything—their parents, their teachers, the government, and even religion. Why? So they could ditch school, go to Woodstock, smoke weed, partake in the "sexual revolution," and dodge the draft. Adults at the time feared the worst and thought this could have a generational impact on the future of the country (they were right).

The outrage at the time reminds me of the scandal around Elvis's appearance on *The Ed Sullivan Show* in 1956. That's the infamous performance where Elvis was warned not to perform his new style of dancing. As we all know, Elvis did it anyway and became a rock music icon and maybe a bit of a spark. I'm not drawing a direct line between the dancing of The King and Cardi B, but I'm just saying that maybe if we nipped it in the bud (as Barney Fife would say), we wouldn't be where we are today.

Now, let me clarify a few things: I'm a big Elvis fan and might be an old soul, but I'm not a grouch. I'm simply using this as an example of how far our standards have fallen. There was public outrage in the streets over a man from Memphis moving his hips,[5] and in 2020, the song "WAP" debuted at #1 on the Billboard Top 100 Charts.[6] What happened to our morals? Instead of the adults in the 1960s saying, "No, you will not drop out of school, you will not smoke weed, and you will not have sex with whomever and whenever," they sat on their hands and pouted, stared in shock, and judged from afar.

Well, this time around, adults—and more specifically, parents—shouldn't be in shock. We are still suffering the effects of the previous hippie era. What happened then continues today. Let's not allow another generation to be lost to the Left. Instead, let's instill good, strong values in America's youth from an early age. That starts in the homes led by dads and moms of virtue and in Jewish synagogues and Christian churches (because any place else runs the risk of Marxist ideology perverting another generation).

We have seen the consequences of bad parenting. Gone are the days of dads and moms living selfishly at the expense of their children's future. Gone are the days of dads and moms who were too scared to raise their children with morals out of fear they would lose their kids. We must revive a culture where having standards and morals are embraced, not frowned upon.

A generation with high standards rooted in Christian conservative morals—whether you believe in God or not—is guaranteed to be a generation that can set America back on track to long-term success.

CHAPTER 4

The Media and Their Shiny Objects

Whoever would overthrow the liberty of a nation must begin by subduing the freeness of speech.
—SILENCE DOGOOD

I t was the early hours of November 9, 2016.

At 1:35 a.m., Donald Trump, a businessman turned TV star, clinched the major swing state of Pennsylvania. It looked nearly impossible for Hillary Clinton to move back into 1600 Pennsylvania Avenue.

The morning of November 8, as polls opened, the *New York Times* gave Clinton an 85 percent chance of winning the presidency.[1] It's fair to say nobody, not even the people in the Trump campaign war room, expected the night to go quite like this.

At 2:07 a.m., Clinton sent John Podesta, her presidential campaign chairman, out to tell her ballroom of adoring fans— who at the beginning of the night were singing and dancing but were now all but in tears—that it was time to go home and let them "get these votes counted."[2] The Clinton machine, and every part of the Washington establishment that promoted her, was facing a real problem. A "real estate mogul" was one state away from moving out of his penthouse and into the people's house, but Clinton's camp wasn't ready to call and concede.

Twenty-three minutes later, as swarms of supporters in "I'm With Her" t-shirts filed out of the event center hosting the "Clinton for President" campaign party, it was all over. Trump won Wisconsin, and its ten electoral votes, to push him over the edge to 270.

Donald J. Trump went on stage twenty minutes later, saying, "Sorry to keep you waiting, complicated business. Thank you very much." And with that, the American people had chosen, and he was on his way to becoming the forty-fifth President of the United States. And since that moment—2:50 a.m.—the media hasn't recovered.[3]

I was watching the media broadcasts earlier that night. It was during this election cycle that I first became interested in politics. When I went to bed, Clinton was in the lead. (It was a school night, after all, and 3:00 a.m. is way too late for a fourth grader to be up.) The first thing I asked when my mom woke me up the next morning was, "Did she win?"

The day before, on election day, my teachers held a mock election in the school's library. Trump won overwhelmingly, but that was in the deep south. Nobody expected to wake up to the news of President-Elect Trump—especially the media.

The "free press" has served a noble cause for hundreds of years in America, and there are dozens of examples of the media and their coverage of significant events. But there has always been a tension between the messaging that comes out of the media and their civic responsibility to deliver "the news."

My grandparents remember Walter Cronkite's coverage of the assassination of John F. Kennedy, and a few years later, they sat around their box TV set to watch the grainy images being relayed back from the moon.

My parents remember the aerial coverage of the pursuit of O. J. Simpson's white Ford Bronco, the in-depth reporting on the war in Iraq, and the striking footage of 9/11.

Me? My first memory of being glued to significant news coverage was election night in 2016. Little did I know how much that coverage would shift the political landscape for years to come.

For better or for worse, the media has always been consumed by shiny objects, whether they are distracted by them or use them to distract us. And recently, they have become deranged by their failure to protect Bill and Hillary Clinton from the American voters, and ever since, they have been trying to shine their tarnished reputation amongst their peers. The result? They often lie, collude, and refuse to do their jobs. The mainstream media in America has, almost entirely, become social activists with an agenda instead of ethical seekers of truth. This is why I got involved in politics in the first place.

The Creation of *The Truth Gazette*

I will forever vividly remember the morning a few months
later, at the age of eleven, when I became fed up with the lies
and the attacks on America, with Donald Trump taking all the
punches. It was a Saturday; I was at my grandfather's house,
and I had had enough. Right there, on his couch, I pulled out
my computer and opened a Word document. I said if the adults
weren't going to do something, I would have to take action.

The media's negative coverage of the country in general
was fear-porn; it was clickbait. Long gone were the headlines
inviting Americans to enjoy facts about noteworthy events, all
there was was harsh remark after scary headline after accusa-
tion. Don't believe me? Here are some headlines from the first
six months of Trump's presidency from some of the biggest,
most serious news outlets in America (not satire sites):

- "Trump's America Is a Rotten Place"[4]—the
  Washington Post, January 20, 2017
- "Trump and the Parasitic Presidency"[5]—the *New
  York Times*, March 13, 2017
- "Trump the Troll"[6]—*Politico*, May 24, 2017

Harvard's Kennedy Schools reported that "Trump's coverage
during his first 100 days set a new standard for negativity."[7]
Their study on the headlines discussing Trump's first one
hundred days at 1600 Pennsylvania Avenue found that 80
percent of the coverage was negative.[8] For context, his pre-
decessor's first one hundred days only got 41 percent negative coverage, and the most recent Republican chief executive
before Trump only received 57 percent negative coverage.[9]

Aside from the negative Trump coverage, I was tired of the media attempting to blind the American people with their own hatred of conservatives like me, my mom and dad, and all of my friends' families. And I wanted to do something about it. But what could a fourth grader do? At eleven years old, I couldn't vote. And unless my classroom needed a new hall monitor, I couldn't run for office. So I did the next best thing—voice my opinions—which led to my founding a news service.

I started this chapter by quoting Silence Dogood. Many of you may recognize this name as it is mentioned frequently in one of my favorite modern movies, *National Treasure*. Again and again, the protagonists who are trying to save the United States Declaration of Independence reference the "Silence Dogood letters." These letters are not fiction from Hollywood but were written in 1722 by Benjamin Franklin under the pen name *Silence Dogood*.

At the age of sixteen (16!), Franklin created an alter-ego, Silence Dogood, to submit letters to *The New-England Courant* for publication. In one of the letters, he exposed an ongoing attack on freedom in America at the hands of those who had the power to shut down free speech, eliminate dissent, and cancel those who caused trouble for the rich. Why the rich? Because as George Bernard Shaw said,

> As people get their opinions so largely from the newspapers they read, the corruption of the schools would not matter so much if the Press were free. But the Press is not free. As it costs at least a quarter of a million of money to establish a daily newspaper in London, the

newspapers are owned by rich men. And they depend
on the advertisements of other rich men. Editors and
journalists who express opinions in print that are
opposed to the interests of the rich are dismissed and
replaced by subservient ones.[10]

Now, before you go and cancel me for quoting a man who
was known at times to be friendly to socialists and Marxists,
as I mentioned in the introduction, my fight is with *they* and
not *them*. I don't agree with everything that progressives say,
but sometimes, when they get it right, I do! And Shaw is
right! The elites who own the media companies use those
companies for their personal gain—politically, financially,
and socially. And to work for them, you must comply with
them.

Modern Media

Let's back it up a little bit. Since the Obama years, the
American media—once known as the Fourth Estate for holding leadership accountable—have knowingly enslaved themselves to the Democratic National Committee and candidates
with progressive viewpoints. And they have served their
Marxist masters well from the cover-up of Hunter Biden's
laptop[11] to "Russian disinformation"[12] by downplaying the
strength of the economy during the Trump years and manu-
facturing other scandals that have served as red herrings to
distract the American public. Meanwhile, Black Lives Matter
(BLM) and Critical Race Theory (CRT) have returned us to
judging people based on the color of their skin rather than
the content of their character.

Whether it's every celebrity-filled DNC propaganda commercial you've ever seen, cringey TikTok videos from presidential candidates, or a promise to cancel student debt—the Left has historically used shiny, attention-grabbing objects to catch the attention of young voters, and over the past few decades, it has worked.

How? The 2008 presidential election was the first one to play out on social media. Everything changed, and we still haven't caught up. Instead of reading the morning paper about the candidates running for office or watching the nightly news, voters could now get their information instantly, directly from outlets, with no checks and balances between the writing of a biased headline and sending it to a phone screen. For the first time ever, activists who infiltrated newsrooms could send stories directly to your phone in an effort to tilt the scales in favor of their worldview. The media quickly discovered they had more control than ever before.

But it's been going on since way before Barack Obama, the Left's rising star, emerged from Chicago and harnessed the power of social media. During the 2008 election, for the first time in history, 74 percent of people who had access to the internet did so to get news and information about the cycle.[13] This is equivalent to 55 percent of all voters in the country, so over half of American voters were getting messages directly from candidates instead of through the media, and the candidate that structured their online campaign the best was sure to come out on top—and that's what happened.

This is the way I see it: for decades, our media's bias has become stronger and stronger, and it's become more detrimental to democracy than just annoying. Bias in the media is the standard, and the rise of social media only made it more widespread.

It first began during the American Revolution. In order to win the battle of ideas while debating with English-friendly newspapers in Massachusetts, pamphleteers like Sam Adams made the early war more exciting and dramatic when describing the battles in their writings. Thomas Paine's *Common Sense* changed the way the colonies thought about King George III by writing things like, "Even brutes don't devour their young, nor savages make war upon their families," as Thomas G. Del Beccaro noted in the *Washington Times*[14] (John Adams acknowledged the importance of *Common Sense*, saying somewhat glibly, "history is to ascribe the American Revolution to Thomas Paine.")[15]

The adoption of the Constitution was the most important "election" in American history. However, the media in America at the time was very slanted. Our Founders were tough and did everything they could to stop the media from publishing anti-Federalist views. In fact, less than 16 percent of newspapers ran anti-Federalist (anti-Constitution) stories. This may have been because of the Federalists' pressure, but it could also have been because they didn't want them to, as Del Beccaro noted.[16]

During the Civil War in the 1860s, the newspapers were much more openly political than the media are today. There were openly Republican and Democratic newspapers battling in the world of ideas and words in many towns.

In 2000, Bill Bradley made a great comeback against Al Gore in New Hampshire during the Democratic presidential primary, coming back from forty points down to lose by only ten points. However, the media mostly ignored that story in favor of John McCain's comeback win over George W. Bush in that state. That lack of news hurt Mr. Bradley's effort, if not put him out of business, according to Del Beccaro.[17]

Why has this happened? Because universities are creating activists instead of journalists. Graduates today want to "change the world" instead of reporting on it. I'm not saying that's a bad thing; I'm just saying they need to be honest. I'm not a journalist nor will I ever be. I'm a political commentator who gives my opinion on the news of the day. I don't report the news.

As *The Hill* puts it, "Journalism is now opinion-based—not news-based."[18] Reporting on a RAND report on US journalism,[19] *The Hill* offers, "More and more in American journalism, we're hearing opinions in news that look and sound more like a 'Dear Diary' entry than the facts of a story. This is fueling mistrust from readers and viewers just looking find out what happened without being preached to."[20] Modern day "journalists" need to be honest. If you're a journalist, be one and be unbiased. If you're biased, be a commentator. It's not that hard!

Who Can You Trust?

My generation is growing up in a world where we can't trust media figures, but this wasn't always the case for previous generations. I think the rise and fall of Walter Cronkite is similar to the rise and fall in trust in the media. There was a time at the beginning of his career when anything Cronkite said would be believed by the masses. He was the figure Americans watched on the small screen to learn about the world outside their town, but something changed. Today, America lacks an ethical, honest anchorman like Cronkite. Instead, our primetime lineups are strictly filled with activists in journalists' clothing. So, what happened?

In 1972, at the beginning of Gallup's poll recording, 68 percent of Americans had a "great deal/fair amount" of trust in the media. For context, at that time, Richard Nixon was president, and the Watergate Hotel wouldn't be broken into until June.[21]

A few years later, in 1976, after the reporting of the *Washington Post* led to Nixon's resignation, the Gallup poll hit an all-time high, with 76 percent of Americans having a "great deal/fair amount" of trust in the media. Today, that number has fallen drastically. In 2022, in that same poll, only 34 percent of Americans say they trust the press.[22]

A breakdown of that same Gallup survey reveals that of those 34 percent that trust the press, 70 percent identify as Democrats, 27 percent identify as Independents, and 14 percent identify as Republicans. Why is there such a strong partisan divide between the lack of trust in American media? Because the mainstream press has been carrying water for the Left for decades.[23]

In 2008, a Pew Research Center investigation found that of the media coverage of both candidates in the final weeks before the election, 36 percent of the stories were positive for Obama, and only 29 percent were negative. On the other hand, for McCain, 57 percent of the media's coverage was negative towards him, and only 14 percent was positive.[24] How can Americans have trust in their media when the members of the press are clearly biased in helping elect Democrats? The year 2008 wasn't the only example of this.

I opened this chapter talking about the night Trump shocked the world, but the reason his win was such a shock was because of the press coverage of the race in the weeks before Election Day. The Kennedy School at Harvard found similar results to what we saw in 2008. In the final days of the 2016 election, 36 percent of the news coverage was positive for Clinton, and 64 percent was negative. The study also found that only 23 percent of the coverage was positive towards Trump in the days leading up to polls opening, and 77 percent was negative.[25] When the American media decided to directly interfere with our "free and fair" elections, the American people immediately lost trust in them, and that's the way it is today.

> *How can Americans have trust in their media when the members of the press are clearly biased in helping elect Democrats?*

I acknowledge there is likely a great deal of fear in the daily working lives of modern-day members of the media who are terrified of speaking out against the "state." As George Bernard Shaw said, "Editors and journalists who express opinions in print that are opposed to the interests of the rich are dismissed and replaced by subservient ones."[26]

Maybe we need more courage, as was displayed by Tucker Carlson, who appears to have been booted from the air because he went against the establishment. He did not cower, and instead of bending the knee to follow the pre-approved narrative, he was fired with his dignity intact.

I was scheduled to appear at a charity dinner Tucker was speaking at that happened to fall the week after his firing. I assumed he wouldn't show up. He had every reason in the world not to, but he still followed through on his commitment. I had a chance to speak with him backstage before his speech. We had met a few times over the years, the first time being at the very beginning of my career at the age of twelve. Fast forward a few years, and he was at the peak of his career, and the next day his #1-rated show was off the air. I had already prepared myself to talk to a different type of Tucker backstage before that charity event. I expected him to be there to fulfill his commitment, but other than that be in low spirits. Boy, was I wrong! The second I stepped through the door to the room he was in backstage, his famous cackle filled the room. He was cracking jokes with old friends like he wasn't the most famous man in America for his fall from "success." I walked over, and when it was my turn to catch up with him, I shook his hand and simply said "thank you." We talked about the events of that week and why he thought he got sacked. We even talked about his future plans, and he was so excited to announce them. I asked him at the end of our conversation for a selfie. Why? Because I wanted the world to see that the man who everyone assumed was cowering in the corner after being tossed about by the establishment was actually happier than ever and proud to continue his mission to expose corruption and encourage freethinking.

Today's "journalists" (also known as activists) won't call out their own party, and that goes for networks on both sides of the aisle. What people like about Tucker is he'll call out Republican senator Lindsey Graham one night and Democratic governor Gavin Newsom the next. We need journalists with that same attitude to fight for the freedom of the press, and more importantly, actually do some investigative work, regardless of if the truth they uncover is uncomfortable for their own personal narrative. We need nightly news anchors who pursue the truth and not the applause of their peers. Then maybe Americans will again trust the media.

Cage Match or Gymnastics Meet?

As I sit here writing this chapter, it is two days after my own experience with the media circus. As I said earlier, my interest in politics was first sparked during the 2016 election, but it was actually the Republican primary debates that originally drew me in. Those were the famous sparing matches between Trump, Ted Cruz, Marco Rubio, and Jeb Bush. That was still when Jeb was leading in the polls and expected to be the third of the Bush dynasty to move into the White House.

Here I am, seven years later, now serving on the host committee to bring a debate to my hometown of Tuscaloosa, Alabama. I was appointed to co-chair the Republican National Committee's inaugural Youth Advisory Council in January of 2023.

In my first introductory meeting with the chairwoman, I pitched the idea of hosting one of our primary debates on a college campus. For the first debate, which was hosted in Milwaukee, I encouraged the RNC to partner with the Young America's Foundation to fly college students to watch the debate in person. This was a huge step in the right direction for a party that so famously overlooked my generation. But I thought we could do more.

I later pitched an idea to the chairwoman to go a step further. What if, instead of flying youth voters to our candidates, we flew our candidates to youth voters? After months of negotiations, the fourth debate of the primary cycle occurred fifteen minutes from my house on the campus of the University of Alabama. When I first lobbied for a campus debate, never in a million years did I even attempt to get it here, but it all worked out, and I got to sleep in my own bed! Roll Tide to that!

But one of the tragedies of the media having such control is that political debates have devolved into a cage match. Long gone are the days of decorum and statesmanship. Why? Because everyone loves a heavyweight fight, and very few people watch gymnastics. But that is what our debates—and our campaigns, for that matter—should be like: a gymnastics meet. Instead of throwing punches and vying to be the last person standing, instead of the bloodbath that is a cage fight, politics should be a civil meet where each person performs their best routine, and then the judges get to vote. Wouldn't that take away the anxiety? Wouldn't that allow for unity and camaraderie? Wouldn't that make the holidays better for everyone (except for the media conglomerates who make money off of our fear of one another)?

In his July 1980 acceptance speech at the Republican National Convention, future President Ronald Reagan stated,

The American people, the most generous on earth, who created the highest standard of living, are not going to accept the notion that we can only make a better world for others by moving backwards ourselves. Those who believe we can have no business leading the nation. I will not stand by and watch this great country destroy itself under mediocre leadership that drifts from one crisis to the next, eroding our national will and purpose. We have come together here because the American people deserve better from those to whom they entrust our nation's highest offices, and we stand united in our resolve to do something about it.[27]

In this speech, the future commander-in-chief envisioned one thing—a government as good as its people. That's quite the struggle to accomplish when you have a hostile press acting as activists 24/7. Until that happens, Republicans need to learn how to play the game better. I'm not saying that you should follow my lead, but I did use a shiny object to blind the media to my advantage. I pushed the idea of youth involvement—which is genuine and desperately needed—as a lightning rod to convince the media to come to campus, and it worked! The mainstream newsrooms couldn't care less about young people getting involved in politics, but *they* do care about ratings and headlines and money and power.

Grace Should Abound

As for the politicians being covered through the lens of the media, I understand that sometimes our elected officials don't get it right, and they wish they could have a do-over.

And isn't this just the thing that haunts all of us social media users every day? We wish we could just delete a stupid post or "unlike" a *like* from the day before.

Ronald Reagan acknowledged one of his "I wish I had a do-over moments" on national television. It was 1976, and he was the governor of California. During a campaign rally, he took a question from a young girl, maybe six or seven years old, who asked, "Why do you want to be president?" His answer likely appeased the adults in the crowd when he muddled his way through commentary on self-government.

Later, on national television, he owned his error. And more importantly, he gave a revised answer, saying, "I would like to go to Washington. I would like to be president, because I would like to see this country become once again a country where a little six-year-old girl can grow up knowing the same freedom that I knew when I was six years old, growing up in America."[28] And then he challenged the television audience: "If this is the America you want for yourself and your children; if you want to restore government not only of and for but by the people; to see the American spirit unleashed once again. To make this land a shining, golden hope God intended it to be, I'd like to hear from you. Write, or send a wire. I'd be proud to hear your thoughts and your ideas."

Can you imagine any politician today apologizing publicly and then affectionately asking the American people for their thoughts and ideas? Well, I can. And today, they all seem to be congregated on one side of the aisle, the same side Ronald Reagan ran to when he realized only one of the major political parties wanted to "restore government not only of and for but by the people."

PART 2
WHERE ARE WE NOW?

CHAPTER 5
Faith

In the founding era of our country, it was not orga-
nized religion but personal faith that brought focus
and unified the early leadership-maybe an unspoken
faith in God, and certain values that came with that
faith. So in that sense, we cannot discount, in my judg-
ment, religious faith in politics.

—BILLY GRAHAM

The values that America was founded upon aren't just dete-
riorating; they are on the fast track to total extinction.

The country that we live in today would be totally
unrecognizable to our Founders. Our modern-day media all
but mock people for being in a traditional marriage. College

students are being instructed to hate their parents and their parents' values. Free speech is constantly under attack. Social media virtue-signaling is spiraling into bullying. Protesters are tearing up parks and looting stores. And the list goes on.

Spiritual warfare is raging. And we see its effects every day in America. It's going to take the grace of God and Christian faith in action to put this country back on track for a prosperous future. And we—Gen Z—can't do it alone, but we will do our part.

Persecution is becoming a common practice in a country that was founded on religious freedom. Faith was once the cornerstone of American life. It was faith that led the pilgrims to Plymouth Rock. Faith is what later gave the Founding Fathers—at the risk of treason—the strength to invoke the inalienable rights endowed by their Creator and to form the idea and foundation of the country we live in today.

Judeo-Christian values were once a hallmark of our great society. But today, many American churches are all but indistinguishable from social clubs and secular service organizations. The COVID-era church closings seem to bother few of the "faithful," who were—from the outside looking in— not so faithful after all. Worldwide persecution of Christians barely causes a ripple in our national consciousness, and it is hardly a topic for the mainstream media to bother about.

We've covered how we got to where we are as a country. Now, before we make a plan to put America back on track, we must be honest with ourselves about where we are right now.

Today, the words *faith*, *family*, and *freedom* are taboo. Faith, family, and freedom are the modern-day F-words.

> *Faith, family, and freedom are the modern-day F-words.*

If you have a yard sign or bumper sticker supporting the above, you will be viewed as an "extremist," whatever that means. Accusations will be hurled your way. You'll be an "anti-democracy, MAGA-loving, domestic terrorist" on an FBI watch list. And what would happen if you were to put in your social media bio that you believed in the value of faith, families, and freedom? The Justice Department might try to frame you as somebody who was at the US Capitol Building on January 6, 2021.

I wonder how many of my peers who are reading this book have heard their parents—and more likely their grand-parents—lament, "It wasn't like this in my day!"

How did a country founded on religious freedom become a nation that squirms when the word Christianity is mentioned? Don't believe me that God-fearing Christians created America to be a blessing for all of its citizens? Let's take a look.

Gilbert Keith Chesterton, better known as G. K. to readers and historians everywhere, lived in the century immediately following the American Revolution. As a Brit, he made an interesting observation about the American founding efforts on the other side of the pond. In his 1922 book *What I Saw in America*, Chesterton explained his view that America is "the only nation in the world founded on a creed."[1] Now, isn't that interesting? A creed. The Merriam-Webster Dictionary defines creed as "a brief authoritative formula of religious belief."[2] So Chesterton essentially believed that America is the only nation in the world founded on "a brief authoritative formula of religious belief." How could anyone conclude that?

One of the interesting things I have learned by watching movies and television shows about courtrooms is that lawyers should never ask a question of a witness that they don't know the answer to. Well, I am no lawyer, and I do not plan to go to law school, but every lawyer should be OK asking the question, "Was America founded as a Christian nation?" Because every lawyer should know the answer. Here are but a few facts—emphasis added:

- "JAMES, by the **Grace of God**, King of England, Scotland, France, and Ireland, Defender of the Faith . . . we, greatly commending, and graciously accepting of, their Desires of the Furtherance of so noble Work, which may, by the **Providence of Almighty God,** hereafter tend to the Glory of his Divine Majesty, in **propagating of Christian Religion** to such People, as **yet live in Darkness and miserable Ignorance of the true Knowledge and Worship of God.**" (The First Charter of Virginia, 1606)
- **"In the name of God! Amen!** We whose names are underwritten, the loyal subjects of our dread sovereign Lord, King James, by the grace **of God,** of Great Britain, France, and Ireland, King. **Defender of the Faith,** etc., have undertaken **for the glory of God and the advancement of the Christian faith,** and honor of our King and Country, a voyage to plan the first colony [in America] . . . ." (The Mayflower Compact, 1620)
- "We hold these truths to be self-evident, that all men are created equal, that they are **endowed by their Creator** with certain unalienable Rights, that among

these are Life, Liberty, and the pursuit of Happiness."
(The Declaration of Independence, 1776)

- "Done in convention by the Unanimous Consent of
  the States present the Seventeenth Day of September
  in the Year of our Lord one thousand seven hundred
  and Eight seven and of the Independence of the United
  States of America the Twelfth In witness whereof
  hereunto subscribed our Names." (Constitution of the
  United States, 1787)

Words matter. And while the style of language of the day
might challenge us today, the power of their language would
seem to challenge us—Christian and non-Christian alike—
even more.

A study conducted by the Public Religion Research
Institute in May of 2023 found that 16 percent of those sur-
veyed said religion is the most important part of their lives.
A decade ago, that number was at 20 percent—a four-point
drop in ten years.[3]

It has been said that of all the models for a good society,
even if not a religious one, the best is one in which the Judeo-
Christian worldview is taught and followed. Our American
Founders believed this to be true. John Adams, a signer of
the Declaration of Independence and the second president of
the United States, said as much: "Our Constitution was made
only for a moral and religious people. It is wholly inadequate
to the government of any other."[4]

David Barton of WallBuilders led a research study in the
early 1990s to assess whether there were any social effects
of eliminating prayer from school. Gathering data from

government and educational reports between 1951 and 1993, the research demonstrated a strong correlation—there was a cultural and moral demise since the elimination of prayer from public schools:

- "Teenage pregnancies have increased over 400 percent since 1962–63, and the United States now has the highest incidence of teenage motherhood of any Western country."[5]
- The number of arrests for murder by teens between the ages of 13 and 18 rose from about 35 per 100,000 in 1965 to nearly 150 per 100,000 in 1991.[6]
- The number of single-parent households increased from about 4.8 million in 1962 to just over 12 million in 1993, at a rate far exceeding the population growth.[7]
- Average SAT scores plummeted from a high of 980 in 1962 to a low of 890 in 1980.[8]
- "Suicides among youth 15–24 have increased 253 percent since 1962–63."[9]

It's not a coincidence that the decline of America in the last fifty years runs directly parallel with the decline of faith in the public square and, more importantly, the decline of faith in Jesus in our churches.

Tragedy Brings Unity

People tend to turn to God in the wake of tragedy. The attacks of September 11, 2001, were on a Tuesday. Five days later, on the first Sunday after the nation was punched in the gut, church services all across the country were full. The nation was reeling. People felt lost. With the smoke still billowing from Ground Zero in New York, Americans felt helpless and afraid, and we didn't know where else to turn but the Church.

I was not born until 2006. I didn't live through 9/11, but that doesn't mean its aftermath didn't shape the America that I grew up in.

Another tragedy happened a few years later in my hometown of Tuscaloosa, Alabama, when a devastating tornado ripped through our city. (This one I did live through.) The E-4, 1.5-mile-wide tornado reached speeds of 190 miles per hour, took the lives of sixty-four people, and caused more than $2.4 billion of damage. Our town was broken. Our city was uprooted and unrecognizable. It took months to make a dent in clearing the piles and piles of debris that used to be the community I grew up in.

April 27, 2011, the day the tornado hit, was a Wednesday. That following Sunday, my church in downtown Tuscaloosa hit an all-time attendance record. Every pew was full, the aisles were standing room only, and still, more people gathered in the hallways and atriums outside the sanctuary. Why? People were lost. People were broken. And during one of the darkest times in our little town's history, people were turning to the person with consistent light: God.

Today, Americans are lost. We are broken. And it seems as if we're heading down a dark tunnel with no means of escape. Today, the people of America need Christians to lean into their faith and grow in their relationships with God so we can help provide a way out of this dark time.

My spiritual journey is similar to many in the Bible Belt. I was born and raised in a Southern Baptist family. Everybody I knew went to church, and most of us went to the same church together. "See you on Sunday" was the common phrase said as we headed home after the Friday night football game or after tailgating on the quad on Saturdays. Church is the culture I grew up in.

I like to joke that I had a drug problem growing up. I was "drug" to church every Wednesday and Sunday, and if there were other social events during the week, you better believe my mom would have me there, too! I know some people just cringed at the fact that I described my church attendance as involuntary, but let's be honest: As kids, our parents decide whether we go to church or not. That is why it is so important to have a strong, Christian family structure (but we'll get to that in the next chapter).

I entered the youth group in my sixth-grade year. That's when everything changed. That summer, outside the auditorium at a church camp in Tennessee, I prayed and asked God to "come into my heart and save me." My dad was chaperoning the trip, and I'll never forget hugging him after the service. I called my mom with the good news, and she posted on her Facebook within the hour to notify all her friends that her baby boy's eternity in heaven was secured. I was baptized later by my youth pastor, Jody, and began my new life with Christ.

That was the summer of 2019, so just five years ago. I am still a toddler in my walk with Jesus, but I've grown so much over the past few years, and I continue to grow every day. Here is the most important thing I have learned: Religion is man's attempt to get to Heaven. Christianity is God's way of letting us in. Having a personal relationship with God is far more important than the box you try to put Him in when you just say you're "religious."

It takes discipline to give everything to Him and put your full faith in Him, but it's so incredibly rewarding. That is the lesson that Americans need to learn today.

We have to develop a posture of reliance on God, not just after tragic events, but every moment of every day.

My youth pastor has a motto he quotes every Wednesday night and every Sunday morning. It's the posture he has created for our youth group. It's even the phrase he's put on the back of our T-shirts: "Easter Everyday." What does that mean? He doesn't give us Easter baskets full of candy every time we walk into the church. It's something far deeper. It encourages us to remember the sacrifice God made through His Son Jesus for our eternal lives. It's a reminder of the never-ending love and mercy God shows us. It's a reminder that even when you're in the valleys of life, God is still there. He didn't forget us on the cross, and He won't forget you today.

I've made a lot of choices over my eighteen years on this Earth. Some big. Some little. The night I turned my life to Christ and accepted Him into my heart, as tears streamed down her face, my friend grabbed me by my shoulders and told me that I just made the most important decision of my entire life. Our country would be in much better shape right now if we spent less time on the rhetoric and more time on encouraging our fellow citizens to make that same decision.

The Sanctity of Sunday

Some call them Holy Huddlers; I like to call them Country Club Christians. Before we can set America back on track, we must do some in-house housekeeping first.

I believe the Christians who treat the sanctuary like the dining room of a yacht club are the ones stalling a national spiritual revival. We cannot make church like a chore, something you do to check off a list. We shouldn't hide behind a social or emotional mask pretending everything is OK or wear our good clothes to church and then immediately go back to living in our sinful ways as soon as we pull out of the parking lot—I'm speaking to myself here just as much as I am to anyone else.

Can we be honest? COVID made us all lazy.

We got to sleep in on Sunday mornings and watch a pre-recorded sermon during any part of the day we wanted, and Sunday School and Bible studies were conveniently offered via Zoom. And all of this contributed to the rapid decline in the sanctity of Sunday.

I know I'm young, but I still remember when Sundays were for church and church only. No practices, no games, no concerts, and most importantly for me, no homework! Not anymore! In the minds of most Americans, it is just another day of the week! It is just another day to make a buck. And for many in America (with all due respect to the awesomeness of the game and the amazing marketing scheme developed around football on the Holy Day), we dedicate our Sundays to worship at the altar of Sunday football (and Monday, and Thursday, and Black Friday, and let's not forget about Friday nights, and Saturday afternoons, and New Year's Day.) Being "part of something larger than ourselves" has become more important than being part of God's kingdom. And church "fellowship" has become more important than following Jesus. And we're seeing the effect of that today.

To repair America, going to church on Sundays, reading the hymns, and reading your Bible app will not be enough. Your relationship with God is what matters most, and prioritizing Him every day of the week, and not just on Sundays, is what will make it easier when tornados come crashing into buildings.

So I must ask, are you going to walk with God or walk down your own path? What does your relationship with God look like right now? Maybe your paths cross each other. Maybe they go the same way but are just far enough apart that you still feel in control. Or maybe they're going in opposite directions. Regardless, you must choose to fully trust God. Your life, your family, and your country depend on it.

I know what you're all wondering: I didn't pick this book up to read a sermon. Well, you got a two for one, because a better America is only attainable through a strong Christian faith.

The "Separation" That Still Divides Us Today

By far, one of the most controversial things in politics is the idea of the separation of church and state. Some will argue that religion should not be remotely close to schools or government, and any opposition is in direct violation of our Founding Fathers' wishes. Nothing could be further from the truth, and the political and biblical nerd in me loves to go to the mat with people over this!

The separation of church and state philosophy was simple: The pilgrims who crossed the pond and whose descendants eventually founded this great nation were escaping religious persecution. They had faced one-religion rule at the hands of dictatorial political leaders and quickly learned that any objection to the state's religion was a crime punishable by prison or death. As a result, the original motivation for the journey to create new communities in what would one day become America was a longing for freedom stoked by the evils of religious persecution.

I picked up a book recently titled: *Worshipping the State: How Liberalism Became Our State Religion.* The book jacket explains the problem: "Americans hail the president as their savior. The government grabs even more power forcing religion out of public life. And unelected bureaucrats are telling Christians they have to violate their consciences and betray their faith. Anyone who cares about religious liberty has cause for alarm."[10]

Writing in 2013, author Ben Wiker presents a history of the battle between the secular and the sacred and how government (along with family and church) is ground zero for the battle. He explains that throughout the ages, political leaders used the church as a tool to subject the citizens to themselves. And he tells the story of Henry VIII and how he may have single-handedly corrupted government to such a degree that church-going people ran from it forever. In his chapter *From Henry VIII to Thomas Hobbes*, Wiker wrote,

> In 1527 Henry had begun seeking ways to annul his marriage to Catherine of Aragon so that he would

be free to marry his mistress Anne Boleyn. Cardinal Wolsey proved unable to secure the annulment from Rome . . . . Thomas Cromwell took Wolsey's place as the chief architect of Henry's policies, including this very interesting solution to the marriage problem: make Henry *himself* the head of the church of England. In 1534, a compliant Parliament did just that in the Act of Supremacy, declaring the king to be "the only Supreme Head on earth of the Church of England . . . ."[11]

Oh, the things people will do out of lust.

Some 260 years later, Thomas Jefferson wrote a letter that referenced the idea of keeping church and state separate. Jefferson's goal was to protect religious freedom from an overbearing government. Jefferson and the other Founders had no intention of limiting people's religious actions or their free exercise of religious influence for the common good. More than likely, Jefferson understood the infamous history of King Henry VIII and how government power abused religious people. And likely most, if not all, of the leaders of the American Revolution and the signers of the US Constitution understood how government corrupts religion. And that is why—and for good reason—the United States is a constitutional republic and not a theocracy.

I have not yet learned of any of the early American politicians who believed that the true religion of God would corrupt government. I'm not saying there are not some who did; I'm just noting they are hard to find.

Not long after the US Constitution was signed and ratified, the states passed the Bill of Rights, which makes up the first ten of the amendments to the US Constitution. And they did not waste any time clarifying their intent in protecting religion from tyranny. The First Amendment includes the decree: "Congress shall not make any law respecting an establishment of religion or prohibiting the free exercise thereof. . . ." The First Amendment wasn't meant to get rid of religion in the country. Instead, it was meant to ensure the federal government wouldn't pick one religion and attack all others. People in America can pray however they want.

Christians should think it's good that church and state are kept separate. People who want to merge church and state generally do so because they believe that putting the church in charge will help get rid of evil. But the past shows that when church and state work together, it leads to corruption, totalitarianism, and abuse.

Just like everyone else, Christians can and should take part in politics. God did say, "My kingdom is not of this world" (John 18:36), and all mature Christians will acknowledge that forcing the religious practices and rules of the Christian "religion" on everyone through a national church is not the way to solve the world's issues. (And I'll take this moment to remind you that Christianity is truly a relationship and not a religion.)

So why is all of this important? Why did I use several pages of this chapter to present the importance that all Christians advocate for the separation of church and state in America? Because we must be prepared to negate the ignorance of the Left's objection to Christian individuals influencing families, communities, school boards, and the country. Everyone benefits when the grace of God influences society.

Don't believe me? Then believe God: "When the righteous thrive, the people rejoice; when the wicked rule, the people groan" (Proverbs 29:2).

I've shared my faith: I'm a proud, unashamed Christian, but here in America, we can't have a "national religion." I would love for all 330+ million people living in America to follow Jesus, but that is the work of the Holy Spirit, not the work of the Church through earthly government.

So when people argue that religion can't be brought into political discussions or debates, that is bogus. The nation was founded on the cornerstone of Christianity because of a desire to freely express personal religion and deliver the blessing that is God's grace. This is why the clear creed is included in the First Amendment, not the Second, not the Fifteenth, but the First. That wasn't by mistake. Our Founders understood that everything else that is good flows from that.

The most important right out of all of those listed in the Bill of Rights is the right to freely express and practice your beliefs because that is the right we must use to voice opposition when our other rights are infringed upon. "Freedom to worship" at a synagogue, church, or mosque is not the only thing that religious freedom means. People shouldn't have to give up their beliefs and core ideals to fit in with society or the government. Today, we're seeing more infringements on our religious freedom than ever before.

During the response to the COVID pandemic, church services were affected by limits on the size of gatherings. And in some states, church services were banned! These restrictions, in the name of "health," unfairly targeted religious events drastically more than they did secular ones. That's why venues from liquor stores to Sam's Club were allowed to stay open, but your local First Baptist Church was told to close its doors or have its pastor arrested. When faith was deemed "unessential," America suffered.

But even before churches were shut down, Christians were being put to the test in our modern-day, uber-secular world to see how "faithful" they really were! Should flower shops, photographers, and bakeries have to work at same-sex weddings and parties even though it goes against their religious beliefs? Let me ask the question the other way around. Should a graphic artist or printer who is lesbian have to make a flyer for a religious group's rally against same-sex marriage?

For both scenarios, the answer is "No!"

A religious group can hire other graphic artists, and many other bakers will make cakes for same-sex weddings. Also, in neither case is a person or group being turned away from a service because of who they are; it's because the service they want goes against the owner's morals. That's not at all like the Jim Crow rules that forced people of different races to live separate lives. During the Jim Crow era, people and businesses, no matter what their beliefs were, were not allowed to serve Black Americans because of these rules. These rules led to widespread discrimination. There was a strong case for the government to involve itself in remedying this state and local abuse of power. But in today's era of "social justice" lawsuits, there is no justification for any government to abuse free citizens for acting freely when their right to do so is secured by the US Constitution. Take Colorado, for example. You remember the infamous case. They took a baker to court because he wouldn't make a wedding cake for a same-sex couple because it went against his personal faith. The Supreme Court ruled in the baker's favor and decided he was protected under his First Amendment rights. The alphabet mafia has attempted for decades to shove their ideology down the throats of innocent bystanders, except now they are taking people to court over it instead of just attacking you in social media comments.

It is also bad for our communities when people and faith-based groups are forced to choose between following their religious views and helping their neighbors. Did you know that around 350,000 faith groups run schools, pregnancy resource centers, soup kitchens, programs for people who are addicted to drugs, shelters for the homeless, and adoption agencies?

Every year, these activities help more than seventy million Americans, and the value of their services is thought to be over a trillion dollars.

In the end, religious freedom is good for everyone. It protects everyone: Christians, Jews, Muslims, agnostics, atheists, and more. People of all faiths, worldviews, and ideas can live together peacefully without worrying about getting in trouble with the law because of their religious freedom. Trying to limit religious freedom is not only an attack on personal freedom and human worth but also on the very thing that has made America great.

That's why the next question's answer is so important: Does religious freedom give religious people extra rights?

No. Certainly not. People from the cultural majority can't use the power of the state to force their views on others because of religious freedom. It keeps the government from getting too strong and telling people what to think and do, which is good for everyone, religious or not. People's right to conscience is one of their most precious rights (along with life, liberty, and the pursuit of happiness). If the government steps on our freedom of conscience, it won't think twice about stepping on our other freedoms as well. That's why this is all so important for me to spend an entire chapter on. If they go for our First Amendment rights, they will go for our Second and Third, and so on.

The Survey Center on American Life reports that in 2022, more than a third of Generation Z identified as "religiously unaffiliated."[12] Why? My generation has a historic desire to be "self-dependent," which is ironic because we are by far the least "self-dependent" generation. It all goes back to the philosophy of being independent and a "free thinker." I agree with that, but when the lines blur, and you see yourself as more capable of making decisions without leaning on God, then you're thinking of yourself as a god, and that's when things get dangerous. So why would a decay in religious freedom matter to Gen Z if they're not religious at all?

And one of the major consequences is that Gen Z is the loneliest generation. You don't even have to read the article from *USA Today*, just the title: "Gen Z is the loneliest generation, and it's not just because of social media. The loneliness of Generation Z reflects not just rising social media use but a broader decline in interactions with neighbors, co-workers and church friends."[13]

To be successful, my generation must learn to have a personal relationship with God (and their neighbors). You can't attempt to tackle the world's problems on your own. God needs to be in the cockpit, and you need to settle in as his co-pilot. (Some bumper stickers get it all wrong.) He'll be there to help you out or guide you when things get tough, and when you're in a situation where you have to flip on cruise control, He'll be there to care for you and smoothly ease you back into the whirl of life.

C. S. Lewis once wrote, "If you read history you will find that the Christians who did most for the present world were just those who thought most of the next."[14] Being a "successful" Christian doesn't mean sitting on the sidelines and watching the world burn. It means bringing change. It means bringing others to Christ and spreading the good news of the Gospel. It means cultivating revival across the nations.

If we want revival in America, we must first have revival in our own lives.

So what should we do?

Stand up.

I mean it! It's time for revival in America. Be bold about your faith. Don't be put in a box by anyone. Don't cower to the threats of bureaucrats, Leftists, or anyone from the alphabet mafia. Be loving. Be joyful. Be peaceful. Be patient. Be kind. Be good. Be faithful. Be gentle. Be restrained.[15]

The key to resetting America is through faith.

CHAPTER 6

Family

To us, family means putting your arms around each
other and being there.

—BARBARA BUSH

When I think of a "Shining City on a Hill," I think of
Mayberry.

All my life, I have been told I am an "old soul." Maybe it
is because I believe 1990s country was the best era of music
known to man and will argue so until I am blue in the face.
Or maybe it's because I binge-watch documentaries in my
free time. Truthfully, I think it is because I was raised by
Andy Taylor.

Every night growing up, my family would sit in my parents' bed and watch recordings of that black-and-white series about a larger-than-life sheriff and his dimwitted deputy. I was born in 2006. The program had been off the air for thirty-eight years by the time I came along, but that didn't stop me from learning just about every life lesson I needed to know from *The Andy Griffith Show*. Whether it was something Andy taught Opie, a lesson on manners and etiquette from Aunt Bee, or even tips on how to win over a girl from Barney's experiences with Thelma Lou, I was raised by that show.

What I love most about the show is the solidarity of the people. And I know it is naïve, but if the simple people in a simple town can acknowledge their strife, name the problem, identify the solution, and come back together by the end of the thirty minutes, then maybe we can too. Maybe if only our nation were filled with thousands of little Mayberrys, everything just might be OK.

I don't think I'm alone in my thinking. When *The Andy Griffith Show* went off the air in 1968, it was the most popular show in prime time, having been in Nielsen's Top 10 for all eight of its seasons.

Wait. 1968? Hadn't 1968, the year of the Vietnam War, become known as the year of chaos? Martin Luther King Jr. and Robert F. Kennedy were both assassinated. The "generation gap" grew larger. The hippies got "wild" and dropped out of school. And people raised their fists in protest at the Olympics. There was a lot of strife and even more problems that year, but Andy Taylor, simple as he was, was welcomed into homes across America.

Maybe it's not as strange as we think. Wouldn't we all rather live in the peaceful town of Mayberry, where there's no crime, no corruption, no war, or chaos at all? Wouldn't we all like to live in a town where morals are still high, respect is taught young, and families are valued? That's why *The Andy Griffith Show* has aired on TV every single day, at least once a day since its original premiere.[1]

Proudly Pro-Family

If we want to lead a successful America into the future, we need to proudly support the most important key to the success of any culture or civilization: families.

I don't want a one-night stand, no matter the lies that are forced upon me. I want a wife, at least two kids, a golden retriever, and a house away from the hustle and bustle of the city. I pray every night to have the opportunity to raise a family to love their God and their country. I long to instill the same values in my children that my parents instilled in me and that my grandparents instilled in them. I'm not saying my parents' and grandparents' generations had it all figured out, but at least they understood and worked hard at protecting not only their families but families in general.

The Republican Party loudly proclaims its position as the "pro-life party." Praise God. But do we need to spend more time being the pro-family party? That is the path forward for not only the Republican Party but America as a whole. We must return to embracing the traditional nuclear family (as well as embracing the security of a close extended family) because it is the glue that holds our fragile society together. But, as we've seen over the past few years, that glue has been "canceled." When did the nuclear family become problematic? It shouldn't be; it should be promoted.

The *Perfect* Family Only Exists on the Screen

Allow me for a moment to shape your imagination in capturing the image of Norman Rockwell's famous painting "Freedom from Want."[2] The family matriarch in an apron places the turkey on the dinner table. The patriarch stands behind her, ready to carve it. An assortment of family members, young and old, have gathered around the table, all with big, bright, gleeful smiles. The scene looks like one that could have been made from a still-frame of *The Andy Griffith Show*: Aunt Bee placing the turkey; Andy cutting it; Opie, Barney, Thelma Lou, Gomer, and Otis all sitting around the table waiting to eat. Everything looks perfect. When you think of the typical modern-day family in America, the last thing you think of is perfect.

What do you not see in that Rockwell painting? A blue-haired cousin screaming at Grandma for misgendering her, a vegan uncle running away from the turkey, or a middle-aged aunt crying in her "I'm With Her" shirt because her brother said the orange man's tweets "weren't that bad."

"A father, mother, and 2.5 children" was once the model of the American family, but now, two-parent households led by members of the opposite sex are not as common as they once were. In the United States, the percentage of children living with married parents has dropped significantly. In 1980, 77 percent of kids lived in two-parent homes, but in 2019, only 63 percent did. About a quarter of American children live with only one parent. This is more than in any other country in the world.[3]

Today, men are chided for their "toxic masculinity" and stripped of their role as protectors and providers, instead serving in media portrayals as feckless idiots. Women ride the third wave of "sex-positive" feminism and are encouraged to delay or forego motherhood in favor of their careers, all the while being told that porn is empowering. And my generation is watching this whole collapse of morals and structure, and as a result we are becoming more and more lost and depressed by the day.

And to what should we be grateful for in all of this? Yep, you guessed it—the anti-God Marxists who have effectively stolen the education of our children from parents and secured it squarely in the realm of big government.

It has been said, "It takes a village to raise a child." I suppose if a mom or dad is missing from the home, or if there are no grandparents, uncles, aunts, or cousins around to encourage and train the child, then yes, your neighbors and your church families surely are best prepared to help "raise a child." But America is not a family. We are a society. We don't have to like each other. We don't have to accept each other. We don't have to affirm each other. We don't have to gather around one big, happy family table. We don't even have to take care of one another. But if America is going to continue to be the "land of the free and the home of the brave," we have to respect each other. And right now, what my generation is seeing is a culture that has fallen so far from the good values of Christianity that anyone who loves God, loves family, or loves freedom is the enemy of humanity. If America continues to go through its national divorce as red states get redder and blue states get bluer, it's the kids who are going to get hurt. We always do.

According to a September 2023 study by the Pew Research Center, Americans are less than hopeful about marriage and the family as institutions. Forty percent of people say they are very or somewhat pessimistic, while 25 percent say they are very or somewhat hopeful. Two-thirds of people (29 percent) say they're not sure how things will turn out.[4]

I am convinced the root cause of the chaos we're seeing today in America is simple: It is the selfish disregard of fathers and mothers. The Bible tells us to honor our father and mother (Exodus 20:12). That's not a suggestion; it is a commandment. Why? Because God knows learning to respect authority—and ultimately, His authority—begins at home. Today in America, we're seeing a drastic, mass lack of respect in general, not just for authority figures but for everybody.

Family values are crucial to a successful and satisfying life; the absence of them is a near-impossible challenge to overcome individually and societally.

> *Family values are crucial to a successful and satisfying life; the absence of them is a near-impossible challenge to overcome individually and societally.*

Family values, when at least rooted in the ideals of American values such as life, liberty, the pursuit of happiness, meritocracy, modesty, helping your neighbor, and working hard, serve as the foundation upon which individuals construct healthy relationships, shape their choices, and guide their behavior. They bolster principles of love, community, and respect. They serve to help unravel the complexities of life. Aside from your faith in God, healthy, moral, traditional, family values are the most important predictors of a successful and satisfying life.

A friend of mine, while observing the rioting in the summer of 2020 after George Floyd's death, said, "When we turn on our TVs, we're seeing people who do not know the love of Jesus Christ and who don't have anybody loving or caring for them." I think he's exactly right. We shouldn't be surprised by what we're seeing. Those are lost, broken people with lackluster support systems around them, if they're lucky enough to have one at all.

We were told what we saw on the streets during the "summer of rage" was "built-up anger" and "long-term hostility" finally bubbling over. Correct, but we were also seeing the effects of a generation that grew up in broken families, was not taught self-control at an early age, and had no training in submitting to authority.

Now, I know what you are thinking—kids not getting enough hugs from their parents, learning the value of respect, or being put in timeout when they messed up can't lead to the burning down of a Wendy's in downtown Atlanta. Yes, it can. And it did. The summer of 2020 was an extreme example, but when we foster a whole generation of broken families with lax morals, chaos results.

Strong Families Create Strong Conservatives

Researchers from the University of California and Stanford University discovered that larger families exhibit a higher chance of having conservative perspectives on social matters.

Prior research has shown that people are strongly influenced by other family members, particularly parents. What [the researchers] found was that family size can also strongly influence political and social views. More specifically, they found that people who were members of large families were more likely to hold conservative views regarding abortion and same-sex marriage. And they suggest that there is a correlation between the two—that membership in a large family can actually cause people to hold more conservative views.[5]

Why might that be? Well, I can think of two reasons. First, larger families can have more pieces of intent or work through issues and dissent to keep everyone together. As a result, they are more likely to filter our bad ideology and morals that run counter to what has been the cultural Judeo-Christian norm of society, which conservatism is closely associated with. Next, larger families are paying for more groceries, more car payments, more gas, and a larger house payment to fit all of their children under the same roof. Most of the time, somebody who isn't already conservative ideologically will turn at least economically conservative when their wallet starts to be affected by liberal policies.

My interest in politics was sparked when I was eleven; my parents could have laughed at me like everybody else did and told me to move on to my next hobby, but they didn't. My mom and dad have spent the last seven years taking turns traveling the country with me for interviews, speaking gigs, meetings, and conferences. While one parent was with me, the other was at home taking care of my sister. No matter how early in the morning I had to be up to go on *Fox & Friends*, my mom and dad would both wake up to help me get ready and cheer me on. When I pulled all-nighters to balance editing interviews for my podcast and finishing school projects, my dad would check in on me before he left for work, and my mom would bring me breakfast when she woke up.

My mom is always ready to listen to me rant or celebrate my day; my dad reads every social media post I create and forwards to me every interesting article he comes across, and my sister is always the first one to find me to tell me how much she likes my latest TikTok. But it's not just support from inside my immediate family that matters to me. My Papa Doug was the first person to forward my 2017 newsletters to friends, and those friends became my first subscribers, and then they told their friends. My Granny goes around telling all of Tuscaloosa how proud she is of her grandson, and anytime I'm on TV, she'll make sure to tell everyone around her to go watch it. My Paw Paw is my ultimate PR man; he made a collage of all of my pictures with politicians on his phone, and regardless of where he is—at work, church, or on a cruise—he's going to make sure to show everyone around him and tell them to look me up on Facebook.

I got a call the other day from Granny and Paw Paw as I was heading home from my friend's Christmas party. They were having all of their coworkers over to their house for dinner and wanted to know if I could come make a guest appearance because they knew all of their friends would love to meet me in person after following me on Facebook for years. So, I turned the car around and headed that way.

Needless to say, they were right—they had been telling their friends about me, so after I walked through the door, it took me three more hours to make it back out.

My favorite memories from the past few years involve my family joining me for special moments. I introduced my dad to President Trump backstage at a rally; my mom visited the White House with me twice to interview two different White House press secretaries; Papa Doug joined me at political dinners; Granny and Paw Paw made the trip with me to Montgomery, Alabama, to hear President Trump speak; and I brought them all to the presidential primary debate the RNC hosted right here in my hometown. Including them in this fun, crazy journey has been my favorite part of all of this. Long story short, my family's support and encouragement are why I am the man I am today and the reason I'm still in this fight.

My family and friend group all happen to be Christian conservatives. It wasn't forced on me, but it was just the culture and community I was raised in. As impactful as my parents are on my life, my views and opinions are my own. We agree on all the important stuff, but I regularly introduce new points to them to support my perspective or disagree with theirs just about every day.

What I want to get across to people—especially my peers—is that you need to be able to have your own unique and independent way of thinking, and you should be able to defend your opinions. You can't be satisfied with, "Oh, I just support it because my mom did," or "I just went and voted for the same person my uncle voted for," or, perhaps worst of all, "I'm a Democrat because my grandfather was."

Growing up, I didn't have to question what a woman was, and I wasn't shamed for my masculinity. My family prioritized instilling morals and values in me more than woke propaganda. So yeah, large, strong families create conservatives. Maybe that is why the Left seems to be so violently opposed to married women having children.

The Frontlines of the Fight from a Teenager's POV

Speaking from the perspective of a teenager in America today, the way women are treated is outright disgusting. You don't realize how far-removed chivalry is from the modern-day world until you do something simple on a date that almost makes the girl faint, like opening a door for her.

A few weeks before that, I asked a girl where she wanted to go out for dinner. She said, "Well, that doesn't matter," and I responded, "It most certainly does." She had never been asked that before. Andy wouldn't have let Opie leave the house before knowing how to treat a girl, but parents today seem to look the other way when their sons lack basic manners.

What happened to decency? We went from a society that measured the length of women's bathing suits on the beach to enforce modesty to a society that glorifies sex tapes and makes celebrities million-dollar careers off them. It is not OK to allow the youngest members of our society to harm themselves. The users and creators of OnlyFans should be shamed, not celebrated. The ho culture has no place in a civilized society. We have to stop talking about "body counts" and boasting about one-night stands. We have lost our ability to blush.

By far, the most degenerating attack on my generation is the porn epidemic. According to Webroot, more than two hundred thousand Americans are "porn addicts."[6] I am tired of watching it rot the brains of my peers and be normalized. I'm all for feminism and women in power just as much as the next person—it's past time and well deserved—but lowering your morals to near the ground floor is not how you get there. And shame on the men who pay women to do so!

Porn ruins lives. It ruins friendships and families. It teaches a lack of self-control, how not to *treat* a woman, and obliterates the way young men in my generation view the world. Forget COVID; this is *the* epidemic that is ruining my generation. Before we succeed in putting America back on track, we have much at-home "housecleaning" to do. We need to stop praising porn. We need to teach children how to behave respectably and respectfully. We need to embrace simple social standards of kindness, goodness, modesty, and humility. Not tomorrow, but today.

Conservative—and more importantly, Christian—families need to live and lead differently. We have to change the way we live together at home. We need more *honoring*, not less. We need to create and maintain healthy families because they are good for our families and our communities. We need to demand and expect moral behavior from one another. We need to conserve and promote families and "traditional" family values.

The key to saving America is that it all starts at home. (And maybe by opening the door for a girl on the first date.)

CHAPTER 7

Freedom

The people—the people—are the rightful masters of
both congresses, and courts—not to overthrow the
constitution, but to overthrow the men who pervert it.
                                    —ABRAHAM LINCOLN

"Can you come speak to my daughter's Girl Scout troop to
help them earn their brownies and democracy badge?"

It was the fall of 2022, and I was on the campaign trail
in the middle of a speaking tour across the country when I
got the text from a family friend who has supported my work
since my early years. I could have easily replied, "Sorry, I'm
busy." But I didn't. I paused just long enough to realize that
I was crisscrossing the nation, urging people to pay attention

to my generation, and here was an invitation to do exactly that. In my speech the day prior I had said, "Investing your time in my generation is the most valuable thing you can do today." Who was I to deny a troop of second graders their democracy badge because of my busy schedule? This was the opportunity I had been talking about for months!

So, I texted back, "Of course. Tell me when and where, and I'll be there. Thank you for thinking of me." And that was that. It didn't cross my mind again until the week before the scheduled date.

I tried to think about how to craft my message in a way that wouldn't put the girls to sleep. The twenty-seven-minute speech I gave the night before to a room of college students wouldn't work. I had to get creative. And it had to be simple. I prepared a visual presentation on the basics of democracy. And when it was time to earn their badges, I showed up ready to go.

As I was explaining the difference between a democracy and the opposite of it—a dictatorship—I was interrupted by a student who was frantically waving her hand in the air. When I paused to take her question, she asked, "Is there a democracy in Florida because I'm going to Disney World next month?"

"Yes," I responded. "There is, because Florida is a state in America, and we have democracy here in America! So don't worry, you'll be safe in Florida! In fact, it's one of the most free states in the country!"

Another girl shot her hand up and asked if South Carolina was a dictatorship because her cousins lived there, and they were mean.

"No," I said, "they have a democracy there, too, but sometimes people are just mean."

I then continued to explain many of the perks that come with democracy: the right to vote in a free election, free speech, freedom of religion, and more. Then, I put a big number up on the screen—the number of people who live in the United States. It blew all of their minds.

"Three hundred thirty-one million? That's a lot of people. I don't think I know that many people," one of them said.

Next, I showed the number of people who voted in the previous election: 154 million.

"What happened to the rest of everybody else?" the same girl asked.

"Well, they all sat at home. They didn't go vote."

"Well, why would they do that? That's silly."

"I agree." I encouraged them to vote as soon as they got the opportunity, and until then, ask their parents if they could go with them when they voted each year to get some practice and become comfortable with the process.

Then, I closed with the same Ronald Reagan quote that this book is titled after. "But . . . but . . . freedom can't go extinct like the dinosaurs," one girl said with concern. "Then we wouldn't be able to do what we want."

She said it so innocently but so accurately that it caught me off guard.

"You're exactly right," I responded. "That's why it's so important none of us get lazy, and we all pay attention and try to save America."

And with that, I left. On the drive home, my mom called to ask how it went.

"Great!" I told her. "Especially the girl who said we can't end up like the dinosaurs."

"What?"

And I filled her in.

The girl simply put what this whole book is about. The second sentence of Reagan's famous quote warns that freedom "only comes once to a people." Once it goes extinct, it is gone. We were not around to save the dinosaurs, but we are here to save American freedom from extinction, and if we can save it for anybody, it will be for that second grader who inspired me to act now, before the meteor strikes.

After that event, the subtitle of this book almost got changed to "Why We Can't Let Freedom Go Extinct Like the Dinosaurs. . . ." but I didn't know how that would look on a Barnes & Noble shelf!

I did not have the heart to tell that little girl, but the freedoms Americans have always held dear seem to be eroding as each day passes. One of our first freedoms secured in the Bill of Rights—free speech—is routinely censored as "harmful," "problematic," or even "violent." (And let us not ignore the Left's absurd rhyme: "silence is violence.")

In 2023, the government was caught colluding with Big Tech to censor American thought deemed "misinformation"—that which counters the approved narrative. When Elon Musk bought Twitter, now known as X, and released the "Twitter Files," it was discovered that the company had put internal labels on conservative accounts to de-throttle the engagement that tweets from those accounts could receive.[1] We had claimed for years that we were experiencing shadow banning but were told we were crazy. The release of the Twitter Files confirmed that conservative accounts that posted certain article links (like the one from the *New York Post* with the original Hunter Biden laptop story) or used certain phrases in their tweets would automatically be censored on the platform.

It's not just social media. The American media carries water for liberals by squelching stories that do not fit the agenda of the "thought police" and even outright lying about "mostly peaceful protests" in the 2020 "summer of love."

Our right to peacefully assemble is curbed at the government's whim while violent protesters on the "correct" side of the social justice movement to reshape America enjoy impunity.

Americans are no longer able to enjoy the basic freedoms of going out in public as crime soars to historic levels and states refuse to prosecute because of "inequities." (Though few, it seems, mind staying home much anyway since we have no money to spend, thanks to Bidenomics.) Yet we will not even feel safe in our own homes if liberals have their way because law-abiding citizens will have no guns with which to protect ourselves.

In modern-day America, our basic freedoms laid out in the Bill of Rights are actively being infringed upon. The issue is this: We live in a nation where our founding documents are not respected, much less enforced. Why? Because the God the Founders pointed to is not respected and not followed by most of our political leaders today.

The Left wants to completely scrap our Constitution and start over. They claim it is outdated, but really, it just goes against their progressive plan for America. They are not even trying to hide it anymore! Every day, there are more and more attacks on the intellect and faith of our founding generation and our rights and freedoms today.

"Sit Down and Shut Up"

First, they went after the First Amendment.

Government censorship is real, and, as we've learned over the past few years, its tentacles have directly colluded with Big Tech to further censor Americans' ability to speak freely. This censorship has even extended to college campuses where campus speech codes limit their student body's ability to express their viewpoints.

What's happening here is dangerous. It is far more important than just getting upset that you can't post pictures of your dog for a week because you were thrown in Facebook jail. What's happening is the normalization of the government's ability to dictate what is the approved viewpoint and what is the unapproved viewpoint. What this is leading to is the federal machine telling you what the right opinion is to have and what is "misinformation" or "disinformation." This sets a precedent only previously used by dictators in communist countries. This is not what is allowed in America.

Why is the First Amendment the first amendment? Because there would be no other amendments if your right to free expression wasn't a right. It wasn't by coincidence; it wasn't by accident. Our Founding Fathers knew what they were doing. Sadly, the infringements we're facing on our freedom today don't stop there. If you can get thrown in jail for a meme, they can throw you in jail for anything.

"Let Me Have Your Guns"

Next, they declared war on the Second Amendment.

Modern-day far-Left candidates, and now even some moderates, run on the promise of taking your guns away, and they're not just all talk. Do you doubt that if they have the chance, they won't kick in your door and confiscate your firearms? Of course, they will! And they'll smile proudly as they say America is now a "safer place" where all the good guys have had their guns ripped from their hands, as they stand behind an army of tax-payer-funded security guards 24/7.

Do you know what their true concern is? A revolt. The sentence they all take in their oath of office, "to protect against enemies foreign *and domestic,*" is what keeps them up at night. They're so afraid that one day the American people will be so fed up by the corruption, cronyism, and cost of living that is manufactured by the people in Washington, DC, that an insurrection would ensue, so they're trying to prevent that from happening by taking our firearms away in the name of "safety."

Now, before you go and tell me that the Second Amendment does not allow for private ownership of guns, only for the establishment of a government-run "militia" (or modern-day National Guard), let me give you a quick lesson.

The Second Amendment of the US Constitution was signed into law in 1791. It reads: "A well regulated Militia, being necessary to the security of a free State, the right of the people to keep and bear Arms, shall not be infringed."

As I mentioned in the faith chapter, sometimes the old language, even though it is in English, is difficult to understand. Thus, how can we better understand the meaning of this language? What did the writers mean when they wrote it? How did the people who read it in 1791 understand it? I suggest that the easiest way to understand its meaning is to examine similar language included in various state constitutions in the coming decades. Surely those alive at the time of the signing of the Bill of Rights (and their children who learned from them), chiefly those who were responsible for the creation of new states in the union, understood the meaning, right? Let's look at a few.

- **Pennsylvania, 1790, Article I, Section 21:** "The right of the citizens to bear arms in defense of themselves and the State shall not be questioned."
- **Kentucky, 1792, Article XII, Section 23:** "That the right of the citizens to bear arms in defense of themselves and the State shall not be questioned."
- **Alabama, 1819, Article 1, Section 23:** "That every citizen has a right to bear arms in defense of himself and state."

And then in coming years, even more clear language was used to explain the meaning of the "right to bear arms."

- **Kansas, 1859, Bill of Rights, Section 4:** "A person has the right to keep and bear arms for the defense of self, family, home and state, for lawful hunting and recreational use, and for any other lawful purpose; but standing armies, in time of peace, are dangerous to liberty, and shall not be tolerated, and the military shall be in strict subordination to the civil power."

- **Colorado, 1876, Article II, Section 13:** "The right of no person to keep and bear arms in defense of his home, person and property, or in aid of the civil power when thereto legally summoned, shall be called in question; but nothing herein contained shall be construed to justify the practice of carrying concealed weapons."
- **Mississippi, 1890, Article 3, Section 12:** "The right of every citizen to keep and bear arms in defense of his home, person, or property, or in aid of the civil power when thereto legally summoned, shall not be called in question, but the legislature may regulate or forbid carrying concealed weapons."

And to ensure you don't think all of these are outdated, let's look at a few constitutional rights enacted more recently.

- **Nevada, 1982, Article I, Section 11:** "Every citizen has the right to keep and bear arms for security and defense, for lawful hunting and recreational use and for other lawful purposes."
- **New Hampshire, 1982, Part 1, Article 2-a:** "All persons have the right to keep and bear arms in defense of themselves, their families, their property and the state."
- **West Virginia, 1986, Article III, Section 22:** "A person has the right to keep and bear arms for the defense of self, family, home and state, and for lawful hunting and recreational use."

It has been said, "Before you remove a fence, you should ask why it was put there in the first place." In the aftermath of a bloody battle against England, the Founders built a fence to protect the people. First, they secured the right to self-defense in pursuit of life, liberty, and the pursuit of happiness. Then, they affirmed the necessity to have "a national guard" against enemies, and I believe they knew those enemies could be found at home and abroad.

Now, if you discuss this issue with anybody on the Left, they'll tell you we live in a sick world, and, unfortunately, confiscating guns is what must be done. But it's simply not.

Per usual, the Left is using tactics to push its radical agenda.

I understand probably better than most the real threat we face in this modern age. My inbox is filled with death threats every day. Putting my political life aside, I'm also a normal high school kid. We have to practice active shooter drills every year. That's not OK. I am terrified of being a high school student in modern-day America. Not being able to focus in algebra class because you never know what maniac will bust through a door and gun us down is not something that should be my focus, but sadly it is. I realize that we have a deadly epidemic in America today, but taking guns away from the good guys does not fix that issue. The real crisis in our nation is mental health, but that's the one nobody wants to address because they can't piggyback it with a political agenda.

If the problem truly were guns, according to the numbers from a recent NBC News poll, we should have a bigger problem. "More than half of American voters—52%—say they or someone in their household owns a gun, per the latest NBC News national poll. That's the highest share of voters who say that they or someone in their household owns a gun in the history of the NBC News poll, on a question dating back to 1999."[2]

Too Big to Fail, but Not Yet Big Enough

Another right being eroded—and one that would make George Washington squirm in his grave—is the modern-day effort to grow the federal government, not limit it.

In 2022, I got busy and forgot Halloween was coming up. The morning of October 31, I tried to think of the scariest thing I could create. A light bulb went off in my head. I printed out Ronald Reagan's famous quote: "The nine most terrifying words in the English language are 'I'm from the government, and I'm here to help,'" and taped it to my shirt. All night, adults familiar with the quote smiled and laughed. But it also brought up an uneasy feeling after the laughing subsided that Reagan was right, and his words still ring true today.

The irony is that a country founded on state rights and lower taxes has completely flipped to support the opposite. Today, big government has raised taxes significantly with no sign of stopping anytime soon, and states' rights are laughed at by DC bureaucrats. They have all the power, not you, and they want to make sure you know it.

Recently, I have been learning about the "Article V Movement" in America. This grass-roots effort is comprised of many people who understand that the states have the right to fix the federal government. Not only that, but the state legislatures, some would say, are the de facto board of directors of the federal government. Where does this idea come from? Directly from Article V of the United States Constitution, which explains how to fix the government when something goes wrong:

> The Congress, whenever two thirds of both Houses shall deem it necessary, shall propose Amendments to this Constitution, or, on the Application of the Legislatures of two thirds of the several States, shall call a Convention for proposing Amendments, which, in either Case, shall be valid to all Intents and Purposes, as Part of this Constitution, when ratified by the Legislatures of three fourths of the several States, or by Conventions in three fourths thereof, as the one or the other Mode of Ratification may be proposed by the Congress. . . .

The federal government was created by the states. The federal government is part of a compound republic where "the supreme power lies in a body of citizens who are entitled to vote for officers and representatives responsible to them."[3] And one of the ways citizens can wield their power is through their elected representatives in the US Congress and their state legislatures to amend the US Constitution to fix government as needed.

If you could change one thing in Washington, DC, what would it be?

"Just one?" I hear you asking.

Yes, just one. Would you reduce taxes to save families money and curb political favors to big donors? Would you eliminate certain departments of the executive branch or change the number of justices on the Supreme Court? Maybe you are watching the president fall up the stairs and think it is long past time for term limits or age limits for elected officials. Perhaps your one thing might have to do with the tension between a person's right to life and a woman's "right to choose." Whatever you think should happen can happen, and the more than seven thousand representatives in the state legislatures from Boston to Austin and Denver to Des Moines can do it. They have the constitutional authority to fix the federal government by proposing and ratifying amendments to the US Constitution.

The US Constitution has been amended twenty-seven times. The first ten times happened all at once and is referred to as the Bill of Rights. It most recently happened in 1992 when the US Congress ratified the Congressional Compensation Act of 1789, which reads, "No law, varying the compensation for the services of the Senators and Representatives, shall take effect until an election of Representatives shall have intervened." In effect, this law makes it impossible for Congress to give themselves a pay raise without going through the election cycle every two years!

How did this come to be? Well, it's one of my favorite stories!

In 1982, Gregory Watson, a nineteen-year-old sophomore at the University of Texas, discovered the 1789 act that had been proposed but not passed and argued that it could be. He started a nationwide campaign to reduce corruption in the legislative branch, and the American people won![4] Mr. Watson, if you are reading this book, I'd like to invite you to become an honorary member of Gen Z! We salute you and follow in your footsteps!

Speaking of corruption in government and its continued growth in size and scope, the COVID-19 era is a perfect example. The year they locked us all into our homes and attempted to force us to take the jab was the year they wanted to remind you who was boss. I will always vividly remember the last day of school before COVID.

I was sitting in science class, and I got a press release in my inbox from the Alabama governor's office. The first COVID case in our state had just been announced. Within the hour, we got an email from the school saying spring break was going to be extended by a week. I remember my only concern at the time was the middle school spring dance. I had already asked a girl, we had picked the theme to be the USA, and I had boxes of flags and patriotic decorations being delivered that day. What were we going to do?

Little did I know that was going to be the least of my concerns that year. My last memory of that day is my best friend and I walking down the hallway to carpool and talking about everything we could do with two weeks of no school. We were so excited. That was the last time I saw him until the fall.

The next few agonizing months consisted of online classes and no interaction with the outside world except through a phone screen. (A study will be done twenty years from now that will show just how much that negatively affected my generation mentally, emotionally, and educationally.)

The draconian lockdowns of 2020 were a direct infringement on our liberties. This past Thanksgiving in 2023, after everybody sat down at the table and began to eat, I looked up and glanced around the table. "Thankful" is the only word I could use to describe that feeling, as cheesy as it might be. It hit me then that three years ago, those same people couldn't sit around that same table with me without getting arrested for going over the limit of holiday guests allowed by DC politicians. And that was just part of the effort to control us.

You got fired if you didn't roll up your sleeves and take an experimental shot.

You were selfish if you didn't put a diaper on your face when you walked out of the house.

You were a dangerous conspiracy theorist if you questioned why that same diaper was safe to be pulled down while eating.

And don't even think about asking your doctor for Ivermectin if you get diagnosed with COVID. They'll just send you to the closest insane asylum and ban Joe Rogan's podcast from your phone.

COVID made us numb to our freedoms being stripped away, and we're still suffering the effects of that today.

How do we get back to living out the full freedom our Founding Fathers wrote into existence? What even is *freedom*?

In his farewell address as he left the White House, President Reagan answered this question. He reflected on an incident in the 1980s in the South China Sea when the aircraft carrier *Midway* came across a cramped and leaky boat of refugees from Indochina.[5] As the refugees spotted the carrier making its way towards them, one man called out, "Hello American Sailor. Hello Freedom Man."

Re-read that one more time:

"Hello American Sailor. Hello Freedom Man."

> *Freedom is more than just a seven-letter word. It's more than an idea. It's a way of life.*

I get chills every time I think of that story. Reagan called it a "small moment with a big meaning." It perfectly captured what America symbolized to the world: freedom.

Freedom is more than just a seven-letter word. It's more than an idea. It's a way of life.

When you think of freedom, you think of everything that makes up the Fourth of July. You think of fireworks and never-ending beach days, hamburgers and BBQs, and even Joey Chestnut and his hot-dog-eating record. Why? Because those are all examples of the privileges we have as free citizens. Our minds immediately go to the extreme, and the Fourth of July is all of that wrapped up in a bow.

The next thing I think of is our history. First, the brave men and women who fought for and defended this great nation for nearly 250 years. Then, I think about how much we've overcome as a nation. This was an experiment that nobody thought would last, but after countless wars, crises, and even pandemics, we're still standing strong today as the superpower of the world. How? Because of freedom.

The Buy-in for Freedom

I was president-elect of my school's student government association, and one of my first tasks going into my term was to sit in on the interviews for our next high school division dean. The person I was most impressed with—and cast my vote for—got the job. I remember talking with him over the summer before our student body would meet him and discussing the changes that would be made for the upcoming year. My question to him was simple and direct: "This is all great, but how are you going to get an entire high school of students to respect a newcomer enough to follow your rules?"

"By creating buy-in for them," he responded, and that's exactly what he did. He hosted a back-to-school grill-out with each grade, hanging out with them in a casual setting in our school's pavilion. No academic talk. No presentation on the new dress code. No update on new rules for the new school year. Instead, he told everybody about his former life as a surfer, his favorite stories from traveling the globe, and shared some golf advice.

The grill-out was effective. He had created a genuine bond with the student body. Nothing phony, just true conversations as he got to know everybody, and more importantly, they got to know him. Then, school started.

On the first day of my junior year, on my first day as SGA president and his first day as our division dean, he told me he was going to meet one-on-one with every single student over the next few weeks. "That's crazy," I said. "How are you going to manage that?"

"By being thoughtful with my conversations," he responded.

And again, that's exactly what he did.

He invited each student into his office for individual conversations. He asked them questions and let them ask him some. He asked for feedback and ideas and wrote them down. He wanted each person to understand their value in the greater scheme of life. He wanted each student to understand the role they played in what they put in and what they got out of school. And then, once he had held conversations with every single student, he called an assembly and went through the new rules, and guess what? There were no boos in the audience—no opposition at all. His plan worked! Everybody followed the new dress code, they abided by the new rules he enforced, and there were no mass walkouts during class or picketing in the lunchroom. How did he do it? By creating buy-in. By helping each student understand their individual importance.

I learned something valuable by watching him lead by learning. Students are people. Change is hard. Patience is key. Buy-in is critical. Now, I am not suggesting we go all-in on a national dress code, but in America, if we want to lead the way in positive change, we have to get people to once again buy into the American Dream.

The American Dream

A November 2023 poll funded by the *Wall Street Journal* and conducted by NORC of the University of Chicago found that only 36 percent of Americans said the American Dream—if you work hard, you'll get ahead—still holds true. In 2012, that number was at 53 percent, and in 2016, that number was at 48 percent.[6]

Why is the American Dream's stock plummeting?

Another *Wall Street Journal* headline for that poll reads, "American Dream Has Turned Elusive."[7] That's just not the case; Americans are just not looking for it.

People today will tell you the American Dream is dead. No, the American Dream is alive and well. It is how an eleven-year-old white, straight male at the bottom of the DEI totem pole, whose mother is a teacher and whose father is in construction, is making a career in political commentary and wrote this book you're reading today. The problem isn't with the American Dream; it's our perception of the American Dream.

When people think of the American Dream today, they think of a sappy, feel-good movie. They think of a picture-perfect story of a poor family on a farm making it big and moving to a big city. That's great—and that happens—but that is not the everyday American Dream.

The American Dream is the idea that if you work hard enough, regardless of your background, you can achieve it. It's not a handout. It's the idea that you are not entitled to anything, but you can earn anything. The American Dream requires hard work, discipline, and determination because that is America. That is the America our Founders created, and while much has changed since then, that is the same America we live in today.

Before we attempt to revive patriotism in my generation, we must first give them a reason to be patriotic. The American Dream is that reason. It was reason enough for the fifty-six patriots to sign their death warrant back in 1776, and it is more than enough reason to inspire my generation to save America today.

Ronald Reagan, much like my high school division dean, listened to the people he served. He listened to the cry of the American people as they battled against the system and bureaucracy of government that was keeping them down. Not only was he "the Great Communicator," which presumes eloquence in speech, but he was also a great listener.

In an address to the nation on the economy in 1982, he reiterated the promise of America to its people: "The dreams of people may differ, but everyone wants their dreams to come true. Not everybody aspires to be a bank president or a nuclear scientist, but everybody wants to do something with one's life that will give him or her pride and a sense of accomplishment. And America, above all places, gives us the freedom to do that, the freedom to reach out and make our dreams come true."[8]

Whatever we do, we can't let freedom go extinct like the dinosaurs.

PART 3

WHERE DO WE GO FROM HERE?

CHAPTER 8

Time to Get on Offense

*Educate and inform the whole mass of the people. . . .
They are the only sure reliance for the preservation of
our liberty.*

—THOMAS JEFFERSON

Courage.

It's a seven-letter word with a simple meaning: having the guts to stand up for something you believe in. Courage is "the quality of mind or spirit that enables a person to face difficulty,"[1] but it's more than that. It's the closest thing human beings have to a superpower. Courage is a trait that is unlocked when you feel passionate about something that you're willing to defend.

> *I don't want to just salvage what's left of America; I want to revitalize it. To do that is going to take a lot of courage.*

It's going to take courage for my generation to rise and save this great nation! It's also going to take courage for my parents' and grandparents' generations to make room for us at the table.

I don't want to just salvage what's left of America; I want to revitalize it. To do that is going to take a lot of courage.

I'm constantly asked the question "Why?" by my peers. Why is it so important to vote? Why should I care? Why should I worry about politics right now when I will have to deal with it for the rest of my life?

If we wait any longer, we won't have a country left to save, much less grow up in. I know it's a common talking point to say the upcoming election is "the most important in human history." But this election in November of 2024 is truly unlike any other. If American voters get this one wrong, we won't have a country left to vote in any longer.

Americans have a choice: freedom or tyranny. Which do they want to live under? I know that sounds like I am oversimplifying a complex election, but that is truly all it is. Do you want to re-elect the puppet who has ineptly served his party in its effort to undermine the ideas and values that made America the strongest and most generous country in the history of the world? Or do you want to bring back the leader (or another Republican who can follow in his footsteps) that gave America its best years since Reagan?

To many, the choice is an easy one. Do you want to re-elect the party that locked you in your homes for two years, closed churches because they were deemed "unessential" but kept strip clubs open, and has gotten America into international conflict after conflict, potentially risking the lives of my generation when we get drafted to clean up the mess their military-industrial complex has created? Or do you want to re-elect the party that cut taxes, brought record-low gas prices, made America safe again, and brought international peace through strength?

Partisanship aside, the stakes for this election could not be higher. This election in November will decide the future that my generation grows up in. This election in November will shape the future of my generation and the families we will raise. We cannot get this one wrong. We cannot continue our recent trend of campaign laziness and fumble the ball again.

We're Tired of Losing

Do you remember in late 2016, right after Trump had been elected and he started his thank-you tour across the country, he began using the phrase "not tired of winning yet"? It was messaging that continued throughout his four years in the White House because Republicans just kept winning. But then something shifted; we started losing.

I know I've only been at this for a few years, but with so much at stake, I'm tired of losing.

For far too long, we have been on defense. We are the party with "radical" beliefs like protecting citizens against drugs, terrorists, and criminals at all of our borders; helping families keep more of their money to spend (or give) however they want; and not mutilating children. And because of how loud the progressives are—especially those in the media who lie with impunity—we are also the party cowering in the corner, constantly defending ourselves.

If Donald Trump taught us anything, it is that people like to win. And when you are fighting to defend something great—like freedom—it is worth going on offense. We need to be spending every waking moment between now and November 5, 2024, doing so.

We need to proudly share our beliefs, ideas, and stories. We should be unashamed when explaining why we have those beliefs and why we support specific policies. We must paint an obvious parallel between our commonsense solutions and the Left's deadly, emotion-driven ideology that is antagonistic toward God and anything associated with him. That is the way forward.

The liberal zeitgeist we're seeing today did not happen overnight. The Left has implemented a distinct, choreographed, long-term plan to take over America, and it worked. It went from Marx to Stalin to Hitler to the American school system and now to pop culture at large. We can learn from their methods to change the spirit of my generation.

I will be voting for the first time in November of 2024. My generation is this nation's future, so we must include young people in the party if we want to be successful for decades to come.

The Strategy for Success

My generation is fixated on causes. We love a catchy hashtag or slogan to put in our Instagram bios. The GOP needs to recognize this and be willing to talk about current issues that are important to younger people if they hope to engage in dialogue with Millennials and Generation Z. Yes, I am referring to issues like life, marriage, elections, climate change, term limits, education, balanced budgets, and a whole lot more.

Republicans have tread carefully on issues important to youth for far too long. The GOP needs to take a firm stand on issues that young voters care about. But hear me out: I'm not saying that Republicans should abandon our conservative stance on these matters. To win over young voters, we don't have to emulate the Democrats. Saying that we must engage in conversations with my generation to gain their support does not imply that we must compromise on our principles. All we need to do is establish a position and get over this game of ambiguity in which the Left controls all discussions of the problems because the Right is too scared to bring them up.

Joe Biden won the youth vote in the 2020 presidential election by a margin of around 20 percent. Millennials and Generation Z voters, who make up the majority of voters under age forty-one, voted Democrat in the most recent midterm elections.

With 27 percent of registered youth voters (ages eighteen to twenty-nine), the 2022 midterm elections had the second-highest youth voter turnout in nearly three decades, according to an exit poll from the Edison Research National Election Pool.[2] Since the 1990s, youth voter turnout has averaged 20 percent in midterm elections. When more than 30 percent of young people who were registered to vote showed up at the polls in 2018, that trend was broken.[3]

In 2022, 63 percent of young voters (those between the ages of eighteen and twenty-nine) supported Democrats for the US House of Representatives, while just 35 percent supported Republicans, according to an Edison Research exit survey.[4] In 2020, when 62 percent of young people supported Democrats and 32 percent supported Republicans, we observed nearly identical margins.[5]

None of this is out of the ordinary or surprising. The Democrats have had a monopoly on the youth vote for decades, but in the last several elections, that monopoly has grown substantially.

The problem doesn't appear to be youth voter turnout, though that is always something that can be higher and should be encouraged, but more who young people are voting for when they get to the polls. Republicans need to figure out how to appeal to and win over young voters if we want to win more elections in the future.

I understand it: Being a Democrat sounds awesome. They offer us shiny things like student debt cancelation and dangle emotions in front of my generation, expecting us to vote blue all the way down the ballot, and most of the time, we have over the years.

We call the GOP the Grand Old Party. Although many people still refer to us as the party of elderly white dudes, the party is evolving.

Women and minorities won every Republican seat that was flipped in the House in 2020, and the Republicans carried over this achievement when they regained the majority in 2022. The Republican caucus in the 118th Congress was remarkably youthful and diverse when it was sworn in, according to the Pew Research Center.[6]

Conservatives who are defying the Republican stereotype have become more vocal and outspoken in recent years, and in certain cases, they have even entered political races. The younger generation is more diverse than in the past, and they expect their party to represent that diversity.

The Long-Term Battle Plan

I'm not just in this fight to win one election. Winning in November will be great, but that's just the beginning. This will be the first of hopefully decades and decades of elections that I vote in, so I'm looking long-term. I'm not just looking at how to beat Biden, but instead, the whole apparatus the Left has built to effectively train young Democrats through government-mandated education five days a week, for seven hours a day. As the education system continues to rapidly decay, so do America's youth. It's not our fault. Blame the liberal activists we talked about earlier who infiltrated public education to spread their Marxist agenda. The first step towards a long, prosperous future for America is getting indoctrination out of the classrooms altogether.

We must start by taking back public schools from the Marxists and teaching real history and not social science, promoting civic duty and not volunteerism, and teaching how the values of Western civilization (and the men and women who hold them) have saved and served more people in the world than any other values system in human history.

Then, we must take back entertainment and stop glorifying moral decay and instead promote virtue.

In the first of the F-Word chapters on faith, I referred to the work of the Holy Spirit by listing the ways we, as Christians, should approach the fight for America. I want to reiterate it because it is not a strategy but a promise from God: "But the fruit of the Spirit is love, joy, peace, forbearance, kindness, goodness, faithfulness, gentleness and self-control. Against such things, there is no law" (Galatians 5:22–23). I'm sure most church sermons on this verse focus on the goodness of God and the work he is doing in and through Christians listed in the first sentence. But I want to draw your attention to the second sentence because no one objects to the fruit of God even if they object to God Himself. We must utterly reject the immoral agenda of the Left and instead offer hope through faith and love.

Earlier, I asked each of you, "If you could change one thing in Washington, DC, what would it be?" If I took a poll on my Instagram, I would expect to receive a variety of great answers rooted in the love of God, love of family, and love of country. And I'm sure there would be some crazy answers like selling California to China because the politicians seem more like the Chinese Communist Party than they do Americans. Well, I suppose it is time for me to answer the question as well. And because it is my book, I'm going to give you three things I want to change immediately (though I would prefer that the federal government remove itself from public education altogether).

1. There should be an executive order tying federal funding for all institutions of public education (grade

schools and colleges) to a requirement that all curricula be stripped of anti-American, anti-Western civilization, and pro-Marxist propaganda, since these ideas have proven to be unworthy of a free people. We must follow the method of Ron DeSantis in Florida. Governor DeSantis completely rid his public school systems of "wokism" and threatened to cut funding to those who dared to indoctrinate Florida students.

2. We must take a serious look at history courses. I'm a huge history nerd. To tell you how much of a nerd I am, I read the plaques by exhibits when I go to the Smithsonian in DC. I'm currently taking AP-level US History, and it's my favorite class I've ever taken. I also understand that the full history of our country is not being taught. Critical parts of our country's founding have been omitted from the curriculum used by progressive administrators and teachers in schools. There is also an obvious slant when it comes to the way textbooks perceive American history. Political commentators shouldn't be writing history books; unbiased historians should be. If we want to take back our schools, we must ensure the curriculum being taught to my generation is the full history of this great nation, not just parts hand-picked by political activists.

3. Parents must have control over education again. This wasn't even a radical idea until recently when COVID hit, and teachers taught (or "got caught") over Zoom. As students sat in their living rooms listening to their daily lessons, parents started to realize the indoctrination

that was going on. That's when you started seeing school board meetings becoming standing-room only.

In Texas, Governor Greg Abbott passed a Parents Bill of Rights into law, outlining the privileges of parents and allowing them to have a say in what their children learn. This is a stark contrast from the Department of Justice, which labeled the concerned parents who showed up at school board meetings to question the indoctrination as domestic terrorists.[7] If we want to rid public education of political influence, we must pull back the curtain and allow parents to voice their concerns.

Go Woke, Go Broke

Conservatives have been effectively wielding "the power of the purse" (something I wish Congress would do more effectively!) by boycotting companies that go "woke."

I remember years ago (way before I was anywhere close to politics) when Target lifted rules on who could go in either bathroom, and a man claiming to be a woman would be allowed to go in the same bathroom as my younger sister. I remember having to find other stores to get clothes and back-to-school supplies because my parents would not shop at Target.

More recently, the most successful one that comes to my mind is the Bud Light boycott. I'm sure you are familiar with it. Dylan Mulvaney, a grown man who is confused and pretends he is a woman, was awarded the "Woman of the Year" award by a popular U.K. magazine. Dylan embraced the award, stealing it from the amazing, beautiful, strong, talented women throughout the world who spent the year shattering glass ceilings (yet he got his for putting on eyeliner and a wig).

Well, Bud Light didn't see the injustice. They decided they wanted to conduct a new ad campaign and chose to partner with none other than Dylan Mulvaney. They didn't just cut an ad with him; they filmed content that they proudly posted on their social media, and they even awarded Dylan with a personalized beer can with his face gussied up with a wig and makeup and a bright rainbow. Bud Light apparently thought they were geniuses, but they were so out of touch with reality that they didn't realize who their audience was. Spoiler alert: It's not your blue-haired vegan aunt or her girlfriend. Like a rock (and maybe a little because of Kid Rock), overnight, sales of Bud Light, a drink popular with country rednecks and college frat guys, plummeted. Why? Because conservatives went on offense.

They were already mad at having propaganda they morally disagreed with being shoved down their throats, but now the pride flag was printed on their favorite beer cans. Bud Light's parent company, Anheuser-Busch, lost $27 billion in market value in the weeks following the ad campaign, as the *New York Post* reported.[8]

Conservatives can boycott and hit the big corporations where it hurts the most: their sales. Conservatives must embrace this mindset and set it towards winning elections. We must stop cowering in the corner after the Left gains yard after yard and get on offense before it's too late.

Vote. Please!

Let me take you back in time, just a few years ago. It was December 2020, and President Trump was in the midst of lawsuits across the country claiming election fraud. Georgians (like many Americans) were ticked off and rightfully upset with the whole election system debacle. They had seen video footage of suitcases being rolled out from under tables inside ballot-counting rooms after the workers were sent home. They heard of various secretaries of state who were rumored to have violated election laws. There were reports of affidavits of people saying—on the record—when they arrived at their designated polling place to vote, they learned "they had already voted." There were rumblings about something wrong in Arizona.

The wound from the November election was still fresh. I drove over the state line to give some brief remarks to voters.

"I know you're all upset," I said. "I know you all feel cheated and hurt by the system that is supposed to protect you, but right now, for one day, I need you all to shift the anger into going to vote again."

The US Senate runoffs were just a few days away. At that point, we didn't know if we had the White House or not, but it wasn't looking good. Regardless, we needed the Senate. Whether we were going to use them to pass conservative legislation or block a Leftist agenda, we needed the Senate.

Georgians sat at home and refused to vote. Approximately 650,000 Georgia citizens who voted in the general election a few weeks prior did not cast their votes in the runoff election. That included over 90,000 voters who voted as Republicans. In the two races, the vote differentials were 55,232 and 93,550 in a total of about 4,484,000 votes, according to PBS.[9] What might have been?

Let me tell you another story. There was a race between Republican Tony Morrison and Democrat Christopher Poulos for the 81st Assembly District seat in Southington, Connecticut, in 2022. Almost 10,600 votes were cast.

At first, the results on election night were close. Poulos, a high school Spanish teacher, had a six-vote lead. A required recount reduced the difference to just one vote. Even more shocking, local election officials found out after the redo that a forgotten sealed packet of ballots with votes that the electronic scanners couldn't read wasn't part of the final count. They had to be called back to the town hall to watch the last six votes being counted. And the result? Two votes went to Poulos, two to Morrison, and two to neither candidate. In the end, the vote was 5,297 to 5,296 in favor of Poulos. The election was decided by a single vote—by one person.

When you hear someone say "every vote" matters, listen to them. And when you have the opportunity to vote, go vote! Taking a few minutes of your lunch break to color in a bubble on a piece of paper could decide the future of your community, state, or country—and to all of the parents or grandparents reading this book, please take your children to vote with you! Growing up watching your parents vote is the easiest way to then encourage them to vote when they turn eighteen. If they have never been to a ballot box, or never even been to your polling center, it's pretty hard to convince an eighteen-year-old of the importance of taking time from their videogames to drive down the road and bubble in a sheet of paper. This is an easy way for all of the Americans out there concerned about their children or grandchildren's future to take action!

The Game Plan

By now, you know that I was born and raised in Tuscaloosa, Alabama. College football is my life. It is the culture I grew up in. I live ten minutes away from the University of Alabama campus, the home of the greatest college football program in history, so I would be missing a huge opportunity if I didn't use a football analogy to get my gameplan across!

Football teams that have been consistently successful over the years have something in common—they all put points on the board in the first quarter. They start scoring early, so it's not a fight in the last few plays to see who wins the game. They don't save their best scoring plays until the fourth quarter. This strategy has been successful here in Alabama and has contributed to the Crimson Tide's winning eighteen national championships.

In the past, Democrats have often had a massive lead going into election day with early voting measures, so since they know their primary hard-core supporters have already cast their ballots, they can focus all of their messaging and campaigning on winning over independent voters. Unfortunately, Republicans across the country haven't had the same mentality. They haven't used the same strategy. In previous elections, Republicans have waited too long and had their messaging and focus spread too far out to be able to remind hard-core supporters to show up on Election Day and reach out to independent or swing voters.

For years now, Republicans have waited until Election Day to start putting points on the board. That's why we haven't been winning too much lately.

Over the past few cycles, Republicans have woken up on Election Day, at the end of the fourth quarter, and expected to have such a high in-person turnout that they could overcome the weeks of early voting the Democrats have embraced. In 2020 in Pennsylvania, there were enough votes cast before Election Day that the race was lost before Republicans even lined up at the polls on election day.[10] There was nothing we could do to overtake that. Republicans actually "outscored" the Democrats on Election Day in Pennsylvania, but it wasn't enough to overcome their early votes.

For college students still registered to vote back home, requesting your ballot, taking five minutes to fill it out, and sending it back before Election Day is a lot easier than hopping on a plane flight on a Tuesday. Vote early and get your vote counted before Election Day.

Going forward, if Republicans want a shot at winning, we must also increase the number of ballots that are cast early and dropped off in person before election day. We must partner with pre-existing infrastructure, like churches and local party groups, to *legally* harvest ballots when needed and continue to lawfully fight against the illegal ballot harvesting. For decades, Democrats have collected ballots at community centers and city gatherings. Republicans must beat the Democrats at their own game in 2024 and host events all over the country to collect ballots leading up to the election.

For decades, Leftist media have spent the days and weeks leading up to election day pumping out propaganda that Democrats "hold such a strong lead" that there is no reason for Republicans to even go vote. This has sometimes resulted in Republican voters staying home in key swing states. Alabama football head coach Nick Saban calls external noise meant to rattle his team "rat poison." That's exactly what this is. And it is coming from the rats of the Left who are subjecting America and its citizens to its poisonous ideology.

There is also a huge misconception in conservative media that early voting or mail-in voting is unsafe. Here are a few things to know:

- We're three years past 2020, and Republican governors, secretaries of state, and legislators across the country have spent the last three years securing our elections.
- Safeguards like ID checks and signature verification will be required in more states in 2024 than ever before!
- There are tools to watch the progress of your ballot, like BallotTrax.com.
- In 2022, the RNC sent more than eighty thousand poll watchers out across the country to watch votes be counted.

The party's priority going forward is to have physical boots on the ground to prevent election interference. That is progressive, that is going on offense, and I love some of what I am seeing from the new RNC!

Be the Roaring Lion

Alexander Hamilton, also known as "The Little Lion," famously said, "If we don't stand for something, we'll fall for anything." This is the same man who just accepted the penalty of death for committing treason against the English crown by joining the effort to create America. If Hamilton could risk being beheaded for you to sing "Courtesy of the Red, White, and Blue" on a warm summer day, you can speak up against your neighborhood communists.

For too long, Republicans have stayed silent. And I can tell you that Republican strategists are generally annoyed that they can't account for a "silent majority" and can only guess how and when they will engage. Who is the "silent majority"?

The silent majority is your untenured schoolteacher with three kids to feed, worried about telling her admin she doesn't feel comfortable taking the shot.

The silent majority is your dad, whose mother is as blue-haired, crazy liberal as it gets, but he will never share his views out of fear of offending her.

The silent majority is your cousin who made it big-time at a New York corporate office but is too scared to retweet a tweet from Donald Trump because she's afraid she'll get fired.

The silent majority is your mom, who scrolls past her liberal friends' rants on Facebook and refuses to share articles or post her thoughts because she doesn't want to lose all her friends.

I understand the silent majority and have great respect for them in this modern-day polarizing world, but if we want a shot at revitalizing this country, we must speak up now! We must be the *loud* majority. There is no point in being *Silence Dogood* if you never do good!

The Left is never quiet. They'll get all up in your face, whine all day, and even threaten violence if they don't get their way. They throw tantrums in city parks, burn down black-owned businesses without remorse, tear down statues without honor, and use all caps to shout down reason online. Conservatives are not like that. Republicans are not like that. Christians are not like that. But we are too quiet. Edmund Burke, an Anglo-Irish statesman and philosopher who lived in the eighteenth century, famously said, "All evil needs to do to triumph, is for good men to do nothing."

I've already laid out what's at stake in this election. It is good versus evil. (Not the people, but the ideas.) Don't be on the side of evil. Don't sit on the sidelines and watch the final nail be driven into America's coffin. Lace up, get on offense, and help us restore America to create a better, more prosperous future for my generation to live in.

I hope more and more of us stand up and yell, "Put me in, coach, I'm ready to play!" Your family, neighbors, and every person who is grateful for America needs you.

CHAPTER 9

Hard Conversations and the Path Forward

*Courage is not the absence of fear, but rather the assess-
ment that something else is more important than fear.*
—FRANKLIN D. ROOSEVELT

We are the party of Lincoln.

The Republican Party was founded in the wake of the Kansas–Nebraska Act of 1854. Passed by Democrats in the United States Congress, the act was a subversion of a prior federal law that prohibited any new state carved out of the land from the Louisiana Purchase to allow slavery. This new act made it possible for the people of each state to choose

139

for themselves. The result was grim. Some might even say it paved the way for the Civil War.

With Kansas and Nebraska now part of the union, pro-freedom advocates rushed into the states intending to outlaw the immoral and wicked act of slavery. At the same time, proponents of slavery moved into town hell-bent on voting to legalize slavery in the new states. Competing protests became skirmishes. Skirmishes morphed into armed conflicts. And the result was a horrible time of anger and wickedness known as "Bleeding Kansas."

The Republican Party was founded because of hard conversations. The first time the name "Republican" as a political party was mentioned was in a local meeting in a small Ripon, Wisconsin, schoolhouse in the months following the pain of 1854, as the *Chicago Tribune* noted.[1]

What was the hard conversation Americans needed to have? The one that led to the forming of the Republican Party? It was one about slavery. And very quickly, a leader emerged. While running for the US Senate, Abraham Lincoln proclaimed, "A house divided against itself cannot stand." He said, "I believe this government cannot endure permanently half slave and half free."[2]

The Republican Party needs more hard conversations today. So does America.

A hard conversation—or what I thought was going to be a hard conversation—is what started this current chapter of my life that led to this book. In chapter one, I told you about the hard conversation I had with Ronna McDaniel. I thought I was getting kicked out of the GOP for advocating a different path and a different leader. But she saw the same writing on the wall that I saw, and because we both love our country and believe the best way forward is by inviting younger citizens to join the discussion and shape the future of the GOP, we were willing to have a hard conversation.

Hard Conversations Are Hard Because They Are Important

If the GOP wants to be relevant with Millennials and Generation Z, we have to be open to discussing hot topics pertinent to young voters. We have to initiate the hard conversations with kindness and confidence. Yes, I'm talking about life, election integrity, climate change, and other social issues. (Is there such a thing as "social issues"? Are they not all moral issues that have been politicized in some way?)

For too long, Republicans have walked the tightrope on topics significant to young people. It's long past time for the GOP to walk boldly into conversations that matter to young voters. But don't hear me say that we, as Republicans, need to compromise our conservative position on these issues. We do not need to compromise our morals or convictions, nor should we buy votes with legislation as the Left does. Republicans don't need to "win" young voters. We're not objects sold to the highest bidder. Our party needs to sit down and have conversations full of genuine empathy and truth. If the GOP wants to grow the tent, we need to have brutally honest and caring discussions that matter. And we need to have clear positions on issues that matter most to young people without playing this gray-area game; it seems to me that we are allowing the Left to dictate these conversations with liberal talking points because the Right is too afraid to discuss them.

Something I think is incredibly important as a conservative cornerstone value is a state's rights. The Republican Party is the party of small government. More importantly, we're the party of limited government. Why? Because we believe the power should be directly with the people, not diluted up in Washington. As much as I am repulsed at the dozens of liberal states with no limitations on abortion, I believe it is a state issue, so we must go to each state to fight for limitations in their constitution. I think going forward, we as a party must hold sacred our position on states' rights and understand its importance.

> *The Republican Party needs* great communication *again today.*

Communication is everything. We can have the best strategy in the world, but if our messaging lacks clarity and zeal, it will never get across. This is why Ronald Reagan was so effective: He wasn't called the "Great Communicator" because it was a riveting slogan on the ridiculously huge car bumpers of the 1980s, but because Reagan knew how to deliver the truth of the conservative messaging directly to the American people in a commonsense way. The Republican Party needs *great communication* again today.

I'm Pro-Life and Proud of It

Let's talk about life. I will never forget the morning *Roe v. Wade* was overturned in June 2022. I was on a family vacation. I rarely sleep in, but I had cleared my schedule for that day and turned off my alarm clock the night before. Funny enough, the last thing I remember hearing before falling asleep was a US senator on Laura Ingraham's Fox News show explaining how it would be another week or two before the Supreme Court would rule on the matter.

The next thing I know, my mom is shaking me awake. She was on her morning walk and heard the news on the radio. She ran home to wake me up so I wouldn't miss the historic moment. The Supreme Court had made their ruling: *Dobbs v. Jackson Women's Health Organization* had overturned *Roe v. Wade*.

I looked up at the TV screen left on from the night before. The chyron on the screen read: "Supreme Court Overturns Roe v Wade."

After fifty years and more than sixty million innocent babies murdered, abortion was no longer the "law of the land." The claim that murder was somehow enshrined in the US Constitution was brought into the light, exposed as the demonic lie it is, and the new law of the land became the old law of the land, which is the true law of the land. Just as it was in Kansas and Nebraska, when the residents voted to outlaw slavery, the voters in the several states could once again take their rightful and legal place in determining the law, separating right from wrong, and, dare I say, Right from Left.

It started to sink in. For the last five years, I had been traveling the country saying in my speeches and media appearances that I wanted my generation to be the generation to end abortion once and for all. This was the first step in that direction, and it was a major one.

I called my dad to rejoice over the news with him, then fired off a quick email to my pastor back home. We had talked about this day for years. We had prayed over its arrival and dreamed of the service the first Sunday after the ruling.

Next, I called the Alabama attorney general and asked, "Where are we on this? Is our state law now in effect?"

"It's set in stone. Abortion is illegal in the State of Alabama."

That day, it became a class A felony in my home state to perform an abortion. Alabama passed a law in 2019 in preparation for this day to come three years later.

Fast forward to November of 2023. It had been a little over a year since the Supreme Court ruling: Abortion was the #1 political issue in the country, and the Democrats were centering every race around it. In Ohio, the topic was literally on the ballot. The state was offering an amendment to its state constitution to legalize abortion in the state. It passed overwhelmingly.

In the same cycle, liberal candidates in Kentucky and Virginia made the topic of killing babies (of course, they always use language that hides the truth) the center of their campaigns. They all won as well.

What did Republican candidates do wrong?

As tough as this pill may be for conservatives to swallow, I'm just going to be blunt: We, as members of the pro-life movement, did not plan a post-*Roe* strategy. Activists spent decades working to overturn *Roe v. Wade*, and thank goodness they did, but it seems plain to me that it never crossed anybody's mind how to center pro-life messaging in a post-*Roe* America.

I have three goals in life:

- Live in the kingdom of God and spread the good news of the Gospel

- Lead my generation in ending abortion in America, once and for all
- Start a family

While the first one is something I continue to work on every day, and the third one is a few years away from being my priority, the second one is my focus now.

I'll be completely straight up with you: My end goal is for my children's generation to look back on this era in America and compare abortion to slavery as a revolting stain on our nation. Michael Spencer, the president of Project LifeVoice, draws this parallel in his book *Humanly Speaking: The Evil of Abortion, the Silence of the Church, and the Grace of God*:

> Comfortably removed by nearly 150 years from slavery and 60 years from segregation, it is easy to romanticize how we might have responded to the cruel and ruthless oppression of our black brothers and sisters had we lived then. Perhaps like me, you have wondered if you would have marched with them on the Edmund Pettus Bridge on March 7, 1965. We all like to imagine we would have. But remember, those brave men and women paid a heavy price for their principled stand. At the hands of Alabama State troopers, they were met with tear gas, night sticks, and fire hoses. That day is remembered as bloody Sunday for a reason. None of us can know for sure what we would have done in 1965, but history has an annoying way of repeating itself and elective abortion now confronts

us with a similar moral character test. Here is what we can know with certainty; if we won't stand for the unborn today while the cost to do so remains relatively low, we can be sure we would not have stood with our black brothers and sisters when the cost was so exceedingly high.[3]

And this is our challenge for today and tomorrow. The people of the pro-life movement cannot snap their fingers and make it happen overnight. But we can stand with our brothers and sisters who are facing the painful decision to abort their child or love them and care for them and tell them there is a right way. We can rebuke the anti-God, Marxist, humanist lie that humanity has no value because it is just another animal in the long line of evolution. We can rush into the cities as the anti-slavery (pro-freedom, pro-humanity, pro-dignity, pro-love) crowd did in Kansas and Nebraska back in 1854.

This is a long, tough journey. It took five decades for *Roe v. Wade* to be overturned. I'm not attempting to underscore that victory. It was huge, but it was just the beginning. For five decades, the pro-life movement set its sights on Washington, DC. The Supreme Court was their target, and they wanted that decision overturned. Now that that is accomplished, we have to regroup and reset our focus. Now, we must target each state. And while the pro-life movement is fixated on state legislatures across the country, the Republican Party must simultaneously be focused on something else.

It's not news to you that the pro-life messaging coming from conservative candidates post-Roe has been ineffective—it has been counterproductive. Abortion is a buzzword. It's the "in thing" every Democrat wants to talk about, but most importantly, it is what they are using to rally turnout in post-*Roe* elections. They corner every Republican candidate, label them as "extreme," and secure record voter turnout even in the most Republican states.

Republicans must change their tune. I'm not calling on our candidates to buckle on their stance; I'm asking them to do the opposite. Going forward, in a post-*Roe* America, conservatives should be boldly pro-life and unashamed of it, just like every anti-slavery prophet who rebuked "the way it is."

Ben Carson, former Housing and Urban Development secretary under President Trump and world-renowned neurosurgeon, is a friend of mine. I first had the honor of sitting down and having him on my show in December of 2020. The HUD headquarters had just reopened from COVID but was about to change staff and a director when Trump's term ended in a few days. The interview was rare in that chaotic post-election period, but I got the opportunity and flew up to DC to speak with the Secretary.

In our conversation after the interview, I shared with him how fond I was of his pro-life stance because, for decades, he has been saying he is pro-life and proud of it. I told him more Republicans needed to have that mentality instead of being bullied into a corner. We envisioned the day when murdering babies would no longer be protected by an awful federal court ruling and hoped that day would come soon.

Fast forward to the fall of 2023. Dr. Carson had been in the private sector for three years and was traveling the country speaking on college campuses. I caught up with him at Auburn and had him back on my show two nights after the 2023 elections, where abortion was the #1 issue in the Ohio, Kentucky, and Virginia races. (Let me remind you that Republican candidates lost in all of those states.) I asked Dr. Carson about the topic of abortion and what strategy conservatives should use post-*Roe*. He said the answer was simple: "It's really important we understand the solution will be through convincing people, not coercing people."

He is exactly right. Republicans are not going to pull the wool over the eyes of any "pro-choice" voters. Instead, we should be proud of our pro-life stance and explain it. Republicans should be on offense with our pro-life stance, not defense. Candidates who duck or dodge it in debates or on the trail almost always lose. The country can't afford that in November! The American people can't stand for it any longer!

I believe life begins at conception, and I am in favor of a full ban like what we have here in my home state of Alabama, but I don't believe that will ever happen nationwide. We must tackle this issue state by state. And it starts with limiting abortions to under fifteen weeks to stop states with no limits from murdering more babies.

We cannot win on this issue (and it will be the biggest issue in 2024) if we cower in the corner. We have to expose the evil ideologies of progressive, liberal, Democratic, and Marxist candidates who support abortion after fifteen weeks after the baby feels pain. That is inhumane. Remind voters of that!

Most importantly, Republicans must shift how they talk about their pro-life stance. Going forward, we should never use the term "ban" but instead explain how we support "commonsense limitations." We need to emphasize that we are pro-life because we are pro-family and pro-woman. We need to listen empathetically to arguments for exceptions in the case of rape or incest. We have to support medical decisions when the mortal life of the mother is at risk during the pregnancy. And we should all be willing to debate the merit of eliminating elective abortions after week fifteen.

That is how we win. That is how we bring new voters to the table for a conversation. If we leave disagreeing, that's OK, but bringing them to the table is more than we're doing right now.

"That" Election

Another huge inter-party topic right now is election integrity. Every time I've given a speech since the 2020 election, regardless of the topic of my speech, I have had people approach me and say they refuse to vote regardless of the high stakes because they believe the elections are unfair.

Look, I get it. I lived through 2020 and the aftermath of that election as well. That November 2020 to January 2021 period was the closest I've come to hanging up my hat and returning to the normal life of a teenager with no more politics. Spending months of my seventh and eighth-grade years traveling the country on the campaign trail only to have the election stolen was painful, but what was more painful was what happened after January 2021.

On the morning of January 20, 2021, I was invited last-minute to be at President Trump's farewell ceremony before he flew home to Mar-a-Lago. A group of us waited on the tarmac at Joint Base Andrews for the president and first lady as they landed on Marine One after leaving the White House for the last time. President Trump spoke to the crowd and finished his remarks by saying, "Have a good life. We will see you soon." And that was that. The forty-fifth president boarded Air Force One with the first lady to the song, "I Did It My Way," waved at the top of the stairs, and flew home from the swamp after four years of service.

I remember a conversation I had with former White House press secretary Sean Spicer that morning as Trump took off in the last remaining hours of his presidency. We talked about the issues with the election's security just a few months prior, and I said, "Now we can ensure this never, ever happens again." Well, I was wrong.

In my mind, the forty-fifth president would fly home, sleep in for a few days, play a few rounds of golf, and then bounce back. I told Spicer that morning that I expected to see him make a fifty-state election integrity tour and go to each state legislature to work on strengthening the election laws to make sure that whatever happened in 2020 would never happen again. Again, I was wrong.

Instead, he spent four years complaining about his loss on Truth Social but never targeted legislation in state legislatures to prevent future fraud. So now, as we gear up for 2024, the few states that strengthened their security did it entirely on their own. (Which, I suppose, is how it should work in a compound republic where each of the fifty states is a sovereign entity. But I wanted the leader of the Republican Party to, well, lead!)

Regardless of your thoughts on the 2020 election, the issue stems back to the swing states that changed their laws weeks before votes were cast in the name of COVID. At the end of the day, there were irregularities, and those need to be prevented from occurring again. Did those irregularities affect the outcome of the election? The general public will never be able to say definitively one way or the other. Why? The post-election media coverage was the biggest mockery of the American people ever conducted by the Left. And to make it worse, a "circus" perfectly describes the way the Trump team handled it. Had the Trump legal team prepared evidence and presented it to the court of public opinion in the weeks following the November 2020 elections—while people were paying attention to the election results—public opinion on the probability of widespread fraud wouldn't have been subject to watching the coronation of Joe Biden.

So what is my point with all of this? When those voters approach me saying they don't feel confident in their ballot's security, I still encourage them to vote. They have to! Yes, they're right. There should have been a lot more work done post-2020 to secure our elections, but there was not, and now we're here. And if our party's base sits at home, we have no shot at winning.

This all stems back to these hard conversations. We must convince our voters to turn out, and we must do it fast. Our focus should be on speaking to independent and undecided voters and convincing them, but we can't do that if our own base is not secure.

The Green Fantasy

Speaking of independent voters, according to a Pew Research poll, most independents who are concerned about "climate change" are strongly concerned and are likely to vote for Democratic Party candidates. "Among Democrats and independents who lean to the Democratic Party, 78% say climate change should be a top priority, up 22 percentage points since 2016."[4] I give credit to the Marxists. If you want people to be afraid of something, the globe is a pretty good place to start. No matter where you fall on "the science," this is a huge topic, and it is increasingly influencing the outcomes of elections.

To avoid alienating the base, Republican contenders for office must understand how to handle the environment in a way that appeals to independents and younger people while still standing with our conservative principles. By adopting an America-First, pro-innovation, and pro-environment stance, the Republican Party can cease losing on this issue.

Everybody wants clean air and water. Democrats think that everyone wants clean air and water on the other side of the planet. Republicans understand that everyone wants clean air and water in their city.

We all agree there is a concern. The disagreement is in how we got here and the interpretation of the data. Alarmists have been screaming about changing temperatures for years. Some decades have been marked by "a looming ice age." In other decades, people have been scared into fearing "global warming." And now it is climate change.

Yes, something is happening in the world. Temperatures are on the rise. Ice caps are melting. How has the industrious nature of man contributed to it (if at all)? And what are we to do about it (if anything can be done)?

I believe America can lead the world in combating man-made climate change by promoting clean American-made energy to complement our current energy sources so long as they are not subsidized by the federal government and part of a larger cronyism charade, as was the case with Solyndra, the $570 million green energy failure of the Obama administration.[5]

And we must stop using American tax dollars to pick winners and losers in the free market and allow innovation of every type to compete for the right to serve people well and earn a profit in doing so.

The Left will tell you Republicans don't care about the environment and deny climate change. The truth is, since Teddy Roosevelt, Republicans have had a long history of environmental conservation. The National Parks Service goes so far as to acknowledge that "Theodore Roosevelt is often considered the 'conservationist president.'"[6] Unlike the Left, we are concerned about the ecology and the earth and have more realistic solutions than killing cows because of their "deadly" farts.[7]

The Left's solution is the "Green New Deal." It should be called the "Green Fantasy Deal" more than anything else. Prices will rise as a result of the Green New Deal, as will American dependency on China and even emissions. Innovation, not regulation, is what we need to address climate change.

Leading with innovation and market-based solutions, rather than with government authority, is the most effective approach to addressing climate change. Through energy innovation and private sector leadership, the United States decreased its emissions more than the other leading twelve countries combined in the first half of this century.[8]

Leading the world with clean energy innovation and energy dominance means putting America first. The truth is that American energy is cleaner than energy from any place else and that the greatest ways to combat climate change are to innovate, decrease bureaucracy in government, lessen our need for China, release nuclear power, and give our farmers and ranchers more authority. There is no other way to combat climate change, save the environment, and expand our economy all at once. The United States has put a man on the moon and the internet in the palm of our hands; we can address climate change, and we can do so while bolstering our economy.

I just covered the top three topics everyone needs to be willing to talk about, but no one wants to. Why? Because the establishment goes after anyone who disagrees with their narrative, and social media companies are censoring dissenting points of view. But we can't give up. Instead of being like Republicans of the past and cowering when hard conversations come up, we should embrace them and win over new voters in the process while still holding true to our conservative values.

It all goes back to a willingness to come to the table and discuss modern-day issues. That should be the modern-day Republican Party. That should be the message we are sending to my generation. We should be advancing genuine, fresh ideas about how to tackle modern-day problems. While today's answers are rooted in the same truth as yesterday, we cannot be a party stuck in the past and still expect to win in the future. Together, through hard conversations, the Republican Party can redeem modern-day dialogue and lead strong into the future.

CHAPTER 10

Ask What You Can Do for Your Country

And so, my fellow Americans: ask not what your country can do for you—ask what you can do for your country.

—JOHN F. KENNEDY

What was once the go-to spot with walls and walls of DVDs available for rent has gone the way of the dinosaur.

Blockbuster lost significant revenue in the late 2000s and subsequently filed for bankruptcy in 2010. The very next year, their last 1,700 stores were bought out. In 2014, the remaining 300 company-owned locations were closed. Today, only one privately owned location still exists in the entire world.

James Keyes, the former CEO of Blockbuster, says one of the most important lessons he learned from his time leading the company is, "Change is gonna happen. Deal with it. It's not the change itself, it's how you respond to change that matters."[1]

Blockbuster refused to modernize itself in today's world of streaming, so it became a dinosaur stuck in the past, and we know what happens to dinosaurs—they become extinct.

I want to have a hard conversation. And it is not because I am an arrogant kid who isn't getting his way.

While the epigraph of the book and the band on my wrist read, "Don't let anyone look down on you because you are young, but set an example for the believers in speech, in conduct, in love, in faith and in purity" (1 Timothy 4:12), I am also keenly aware of another verse: "The glory of young men is their strength, gray hair the splendor of the old" (Proverbs 20:29). If you are not aware of the metaphor, the reference to gray hair is an acknowledgment of wisdom. The Bible teaches us that in this world, we naturally admire the strength of people while they are young and the wisdom of people when they have lived a full life.

I wish this were true. I wish our culture still admired the young and the old alike. But I fear that without the foundation of faith, family, and freedom, many of us are living out our days looking after #1 at the expense of everyone else. I want to learn from my parents and grandparents and the senior members of the GOP. And I want them to ask me questions and teach me well. But it seems to me that too many of our senior members of government may just be looking out for #1, and it is time for us to change how government works to prevent the appearance of impropriety. What am I talking about? What hard conversation do I want to have? One about term limits.

As of the writing of this book, there are twelve elected officials currently serving in the US Congress who have been there for more than thirty-six years. (And, in the history of America, there have been 120 who have served at least thirty-six years).[2]

And for honorable mention, Joe Biden served for thirty-six years in the US Senate, eight years as vice president, and now four as president, for a total of forty-eight years in Washington, DC. And John Dingell served his constituents and the DNC for fifty-nine years before he retired in 2014.

And people are noticing—not just the terms, but the years. Take a look at some recent headlines by outlets you wouldn't expect to be calling out the establishment:

- ABC News: "Congress Today Is Older Than It's Ever Been"[3]
- CNN: "They're 80+. They're in Charge. They're Not Going Away."[4]
- *New York Times*: "Here Are the 20 Oldest Members of Congress"[5]

A dear friend of mine confronted me a few weeks ago at an event; she pulled me aside and told me she felt it was rude of me to be advocating for my generation to get involved in the party.

"What do you mean?" I asked.

She told me she felt like I was not appreciating the decades of hard work and service by some of the longstanding members of the party.

I want to share with you what I expressed to her. I don't want to kick anybody out of our party—I want to grow our party. I want the current members to make room at the table for my generation, not get up from the table entirely.

Before I continue, let me explain: There's an important distinction between term limits and age limits. I was raised to respect my elders. I was instructed to listen more than I talk. I don't have an informed opinion of age limits at this time. I understand they exist in the military and for commercial airline pilots, and I don't have anything to say about that. But I don't think it's respectful to humiliate people by propping them up to keep power in numbers. It is shameful to watch power-hungry people abuse others by allowing them to mentally and physically decline in public to the point where they tarnish their entire careers. And the mainstream media is taking note, even if they are not doing anything about it.

Allow me to make a country music analogy. (I've already told y'all that I am an old soul.) I believe the kings of country music are George Strait, Waylon Jennings, and Johnny Cash. I've attended two George Strait concerts with my mom and have enjoyed hours and hours of music and footage of Waylon and Cash, along with countless songs from Willie Nelson, Merle Haggard, and George Jones. They sang true country music, not this pop crossover mess we've got today.

But that doesn't mean I don't have an ear for any contemporary artists today. I think Cody Johnson does it perfectly. His music is a righteous blend of old and new, intertwining the classic country style and lyrics with a modern-day twist. (Maybe it helps that he's a real-life cowboy and even dares to throw a mini political rally into the middle of his concerts.) He pays homage to the legends who created the genre and adds an appropriate, present-day style.

That's what we, as the next generation of Republicans, need to do: respect the legends that came before us and bring a modern style to the table. All we are asking for is some seats at the table, but not just at the kid's table off in the corner. We want to sit with the adults and learn from them, discuss ideas, and debate the best path forward.

The problem is not old politicians but a lack of representation of the voters. According to Axios, "The average American is 20 years younger than the average representative in the House and Senate. Forty percent of current senators and 26% of representatives are 65 years or older—and many have strolled the Capitol's marble halls for decades. Less than 5% of members are from the ages of 25 to 40, compared to 33% of the U.S. population."[6] And at the time of my writing of this chapter, the voters in Houston are preparing to choose their next mayor. According to the Associated Press, "Whichever candidate wins will be the oldest big city mayor in the U.S. Either Jackson Lee or Whitmire will lead a city which is becoming younger, with a median age of around 35 and with 25% of its population below 18, according to census figures."[7]

The problem is not forty years of service but a lack of modern solutions to problems (both new and old). Now, maybe if our elected leaders listened to us more or were committed to their craft, like doctors, architects, and teachers who are required to collect continuing education credits to know the latest innovations in their fields, we would have better solutions. But it seems that the only things our elected officials are required to amass are dollars, donors, votes, and publicity, and they spend a lot of time (and way too many years) doing so.

And I know that people seeming to stay too long is not unique to politics. A recent Fortune article explains something similar is happening in boardrooms: "Vacancies do not occur frequently, meaning board leaders must either expand the board or wait for someone to retire or step down before adding someone new."[8] And what are companies doing? They are diversifying their boards by setting age limits.

A lot of the policies and positions conceived and promoted by long-term leaders of the GOP are incredible; these leaders and their values are the reason I am a member of the Republican Party. Nevertheless, some of the ideas, policies, and positions are dated and are a drag on the party's ability to effectively represent the American people.

I believe that we will attract new voters to the Republican Party by spending more time listening and less time talking, promoting values that align with the Judeo-Christian culture America was founded on, and enacting new ideas that leverage the strengths of the younger generations, the very ones the Boomers and Gen Xers have fought so hard to train well.

There is a chance that I'm wrong, but I'm pretty sure every current politician thought much the same thing when they asked for their seat at their parents' table.

Overlooked

My generation feels ignored by Washington, DC. As we listen to the speeches and watch the actions of the parties and the government leaders, we feel overlooked and are convinced we are less cared for than other members of the national electorate.

In 2024, 48.5 percent of voters will be made up of Gen Z and Millennials, according to the US Census Bureau. And 48.5 percent of overall voters cannot feel unheard or left out.[9] It is time for party leaders on both sides to prepare the next generation for success today and succession in the coming years.

A recent survey conducted by World Values Survey found that 47.7 percent of young people (ages eighteen to twenty-nine) around the world vote in national elections. Depending on the country and area, the numbers fluctuate a little bit. For example, more than 65 percent of young people in Latin America vote, while only 40 to 50 percent of young people in Europe and Africa vote.[10]

In the United States, only 48 percent of people aged eighteen to twenty-four who were eligible to vote in the 2020 presidential election did so.[11] That's more than the international average, but that was the lowest rate of any age group. The low number of young people in America who vote reveals the apathy, mistrust, and dissatisfaction that is growing in America. And it shows that the Marxist battle against freedom and democracy is succeeding.

To its credit, the Republican Party has started to focus on addressing this in recent years. All over the country, we have watched young, fresh, conservative fighters elected and sent to Washington, and it's incredibly exciting to see! The Republican Party is truly no longer the party of "old white guys," and our recent elections reflect that.

We're the party of Anna Paulina Luna, a Hispanic American who grew up in a family plagued by drug addiction, was raised by a single mother in poverty in southern California, and after overcoming all of that, is now representing the great state of Florida in Congress at only age thirty-three.

We're the party of Tim Scott, a black man who grew up in poverty with his family picking cotton in South Carolina, who now represents that same state in the United States Senate.

We're the party of Kat Cammack, a woman who just a few years ago was homeless and living in her car. She overcame her circumstances and is now representing the great state of Florida in Congress.

We're the party of Katie Britt, the first female to be elected to be a US senator from the great State of Alabama, the youngest Republican woman in US history to be elected to the US Senate, and the only female Republican with school-age children currently serving in the US Senate. She was forty years old when she was elected and won her primary against a career politician who had been in politics for forty years.

That is the modern-day Republican Party. That is the message we need to be getting out to my generation. That is the message we win on going forward.

Power Corrupts—(Shocker!)

I find it interesting that one of the most controversial topics in Washington, DC, is the idea of term limits. This should not be a partisan issue. The American people think both sides keep their politicians in Washington for way too long.

Let me let you in on a little secret. Very few in Washington will ever release the grip they have on their power. No one ever thinks it is "their time to go." I can't begin to tell you the countless "conservative" candidates I have supported who ran on a term-limits pledge and then get to Washington and act like that piece of paper they signed is the equivalent of toilet paper.

We've all seen the footage of trick-or-treaters during the 2023 Halloween season dressed up as Joe Biden (then eighty years old) and intentionally falling to the ground mimicking the man's frail state. I have to admit that I laughed, but then I was sad because power-hungry people are afraid to say it like it is about Joe Biden. After all, one day, someone might say the same thing about them.

We must be able to come together and support term limits for the good of the country. This should be a bipartisan issue passed without much debate, and the good people at US Term Limits are leading the charge.[12] But asking DC bureaucrats to vote on limiting their years in power is like asking them not to gain financially from privileged information. It's just not going to happen (and that is one of the reasons I mentioned the Article V Movement in an earlier chapter.)

When I sat down and interviewed Grammy-award-winning and multi-platinum recording artist Lee Greenwood for my podcast, during our conversation, he announced his retirement. He said something that stuck out to me. He shared that the most important thing his mother taught him was, "It doesn't matter what you do at the beginning; it's the end that counts."

To remind himself of that, after his performances, he says "ta-da" and waves jazz hands like a magician finishing an incredible trick. Politicians in Washington should have the same mindset: Wave your jazz hands, give a retirement speech, and go home and lead your family, run your business, volunteer at your kids' school, or serve on a corporate board while you are still young enough to do so. But too often, politicians and bureaucrats stay in power while having multiple strokes on TV and having to be pushed around in a wheelchair because they are too frail to move. Honestly, it's elder abuse by the families and those who are hungry for more and more power that keep sending these people back to Washington, DC.

Again, it is about terms, not age. If you're ninety and physically and mentally fit to run for office and the people elect you, best of luck to you! But if you're attempting to spend your life making a fortune off the taxpayers' dime and stay in the game to grow your personal (or your family's) power, you need to go home.

Because of all of this, I would enact a constitutional amendment to set term limits for the US Congress.

In the House, I would limit service to three four-year terms. This would enable representatives to spend more time serving their constituents than building a war chest to win battle after battle every two years for decades to come.

I would keep the senators' terms at six years and enact term limits.

Thus, representatives could serve up to three terms (twelve years total) if reelected. Senators could serve up to two terms (twelve years total) if reelected.

The result? While it might be simplistic, I believe if we start talking about the influence of money and the power of time, many of the major issues we're facing today—insider trading, long-term lobbyist bribing schemes, and cognitive decline—could all be reduced.

Changing the Status Quo in Washington, DC

Can this be done? Could we possibly change how power corrupts even the best intentions of the noblest people who go to Washington, DC?

Yes. If it can happen at the state level, it can happen at the federal level.

According to US Term Limits, "thirty-seven states have term limits on their governors imposed at the founding of their respective state constitutions. Term limits on governors are a common and effective check and balance in statewide governance."[13] While states have varying laws—as they should, since they are incubators of federalism within the United States of America—most have established that the best form of leadership is limited leadership.

This is not some new, novel concept. The idea has been around since the Constitutional Convention. Representative Thomas Tucker made the first suggestion for term limits in 1789. In his review of the draft of the new Constitution, he offered this amendment to Article 1, Section 2, Clause 2:

At the end add these words, "nor shall any person be capable of serving as a representative more than six years in any term of eight years."[14]

George Washington was the humble leader who first stepped down after two terms as commander-in-chief, declining to be a king or a dictator. He set a precedent for the young nation he had just helped create.

Thomas Jefferson continued to support this idea in 1808.

The practice of no more than two terms for presidents was kept up unofficially for 132 years, though Ulysses S. Grant, Theodore Roosevelt, and Woodrow Wilson all tried to serve more than two terms. Grant and Wilson tried to get the support of their parties but failed.

In 1940, Franklin D. Roosevelt was able to break from tradition by saying World War II was about to start. He was elected to a third and then fourth term but died just months after his swearing-in for his fourth term.

The two-term limit was made official by the Twenty-Second Amendment to the US Constitution, which was passed in 1951. However, it did not apply to Harry S. Truman, who was president at the time. But Truman chose not to run for a third term.

Again, what I am advocating for is that those who love America enact processes whereby the efforts of the Washington elite are constrained. This includes my peers. It includes state legislators who have the power to change how Washington, DC, operates. It includes incumbent politicians who take seriously the challenge from John F. Kennedy that we should "ask not what your country can do for you—ask what you can do for your country."[15]

What I'm asking for is an invitation to my generation to sit at the table so we can do something to help save our country.

Ronald Reagan famously assessed the never-ending nature of government control, saying, "No government ever voluntarily reduces itself in size. So governments' programs, once launched, never disappear. A government bureau is the nearest thing to eternal life we'll ever see on this earth."[16]

I see his warning, and I will add one of my own: Few career politicians, once elected, seem to make themselves disappear.

What I'm asking for is an invitation to my generation to sit at the table so we can do something to help save our country.

CHAPTER 11

For Such a Time as This

To my young friends out there: Life can be great, but not when you can't see it. So, open your eyes to life: to see it in the vivid colors that God gave us as a precious gift to His children, to enjoy life to the fullest, and to make it count. Say yes to your life.

—NANCY REAGAN

I'm going to let you in on a little secret: I still get nervous. I do! I won't pretend that when I shake Donald Trump's hand or appear on national TV, I'm not a little anxious. And yes, I get nervous every time I interview a presidential candidate, elected representative, or political pundit. It has been seven years and hundreds of interviews later, and I am still nervous every time a producer places a microphone on me or when I turn on my camera for a Zoom call.

So, how do I deal with this? How do I make it through my speeches, interviews, or meetings without letting my nerves get the best of me?

My coping method is simple: I give it all to the Lord. I put my full trust in Him.

Before every big meeting, every interview, every speech, and every TV appearance, I recite a phrase aloud to myself: "God, if it's your will, let it be done."

I even found myself repeating that phrase over and over as I wrote this book.

Why? Uttering those nine words is verbally surrendering all nerves, all anxiety, and all worry to God. If it is His will for this interview, speech, or TV hit to go well, I'm putting my full faith in Him for that to happen.

That is the posture that America needs to be in right now. You don't need me to tell you that our country is going down the wrong track—you already know that! You see it all around you every day. We live in a secular, selfish, and sinful world. People need to tune out all the external noises and distractions, all the "rat poison" that I referred to earlier, and put their full faith in God.

Ronald Reagan often called America "The Shining City on a Hill" in his speeches. In his 1989 farewell address as commander in chief, at age seventy-eight, the once young actor turned governor who called upon his fellow Americans to once again hope in the future was now on his way out of politics after serving two terms in the Oval Office. He once again drew the attention of the American people to the beauty of freedom, saying,

> The past few days when I've been at that window upstairs, I've thought a bit of the "shining city upon a hill." The phrase comes from John Winthrop, who wrote it to describe the America he imagined. What he imagined was important because he was an early Pilgrim, an early freedom man. He journeyed here on what today we'd call a little wooden boat; and like the other Pilgrims, he was looking for a home that would be free.
>
> I've spoken of the shining city all my political life, but I don't know if I ever quite communicated what I saw when I said it. But in my mind it was a tall, proud city built on rocks stronger than oceans, wind-swept, God-blessed, and teeming with people of all kinds living in harmony and peace; a city with free ports that hummed with commerce and creativity. And if there had to be city walls, the walls had doors and the doors were open to anyone with the will and the heart to get here. That's how I saw it, and see it still.[1]

The future America Ronald Reagan was imagining back in 1989 is far from the one we live in today. You can look around yourself and notice that there is little "peace" and even less "harmony." Maybe America has lost its shine. And perhaps it is not just the fact that our major cities are infested with crime, and their sidewalks are covered with strung-out druggies living off the taxpayers' dime.

More and more, people publicly proclaim they are no longer "proud" to be American. A 2023 Gallup poll found that only 39 percent of Americans are proud of their country.[2] Instead, they rebuke the successes of this great American experiment in freedom and self-government, mock how long it has survived, and seek out every possible opportunity to criticize it and threaten to abandon it constantly.

Every time I turn on the news, I feel like we're all living in that meme where you're sitting in a burning house but instead of addressing it, you just tell yourself "Everything is fine." Well, friends, I've got news for you today—as hard as it may be to swallow. Everything is not fine. The America that Winthrop and Reagan saw may be further from reality today than it was nearly four centuries and forty years ago, respectively.

But one thing from Reagan's description of his ideal America encourages me: He calls us "God-blessed." He's right! We are! Regardless of what war, pandemic, or unrest we're facing, we are a nation founded on the cornerstone of Christianity. A country desiring freedom, but most specifically, the freedom to worship God Almighty! The only way America has survived nearly 250 years is because of the watchful eye of the Lord. That is something that cannot be taken away from us, no matter what other freedoms *they* try to take away. That is something that no liberal activist can change, no matter how hard they scream or what color they dye their hair.

We are the land of the free, blessed by God with the country we're living in today, and no media propaganda spin can change that or make you feel ashamed of this great nation.

When 132 passengers sailed across the Atlantic—from Southampton, England, to Boston, Massachusetts, to find a new and better world—they did not expect to discover the "shining city on a hill," but to build it.

When George Washington led the rag-tag Continental Army of patriots against the most powerful military on earth, the "shining city on a hill" was the infant country they sought to defend.

During both world wars, as the very idea of individual freedoms was under assault by growing anti-God ideologies across the world, the idea of the "shining city on a hill" and its forever companion, *truth*, was what led our infantryman into battle.

And while America is rooted in the truth and morals of the Judeo-Christian worldview presented by the proclamations of the Bible, it was one dream, one vision, and one hope by our Founding Fathers that created this land of the free. That dream turned into an experiment that has withstood countless secular, selfish, and sinful attacks from both within and without. But the vision of freedom marches on, and it is time—once again—for America to not only be the land of the free but also the home of the brave.

In February 2023, *Jesus Revolution* hit the big screens. A Christian movie about the revival that spread across the country in the 1960s and 1970s soared at the box office. Starting in California during the hippie movement, the real revolution covered in the movie was a genuine cry for help by a lost generation of teenagers. God answered that cry, and Christianity hit record numbers, moving across the country like wildfire!

Why am I talking about blockbuster movies? Well, the revival that the movie covered is desperately needed in today's America. We got a little taste of it last year!

In that same month, at a tiny Christian college in Kentucky tucked in an even smaller chapel, a revival began. After an ordinary Wednesday night campus church service, a few students decided to keep praying and worshiping—and they didn't stop.

At first, the only people aware of this interruption to the school's schedule were the locals. By the fourth day, media interest had significantly increased, and all anybody was talking about anywhere were the events at Asbury University. Videos of the never-ending service went viral on social media, and soon, lines formed outside the doors of the small chapel where people waited dozens of hours, if not days in some cases, to be part of the moment.[3]

Just like that, sixty to seventy years after the hippie revival of the twentieth century, revival started again, and just like last time, it spread like wildfire.

And people were not satisfied just watching the revival contained within the Asbury University campus; all across the country, churches, colleges, sporting arenas—anywhere big enough to hold a crowd—were filled with hungry Christians wanting something new, something less worldly. They wanted something heavenly, and they sought a glimpse of God's shining city!

It seems to me that when the world hits rock bottom, historically, revival follows. Revivals throughout history tend to happen when people are grasping in the dark for something substantial in their lives, something of meaning and, dare I say, something of eternal value. From the Great Awakenings shepherded by George Whitefield, Jonathan Edwards, and Gilbert Tennent that started in the 1700s, to the sounds of freedom sung in black churches across America following the end of chattel slavery in America in the 1800s, to the cheers of millions at the news of the overturning of the evil consequences of *Roe v. Wade*, and a thousand times in between, revivals have stirred faithful men and women of God to do what is right in the eyes of the Lord and for their neighbors.

At the time of the Asbury Revival, three years after government responses to the global pandemic shut down everything, our freedoms were stripped from us, inflation soared through the roof, and riots and violence in the streets were a nightly scheduled TV program, it looked pretty much like America had hit that rocky bottom floor. And a flame lit in a chapel on a college campus caused revival to glow once again in the shining city on a hill.

Similar to the spiritual revival in the 1960s and 1970s, the 2023 Asbury Revival was started by kids. What happened at Asbury was my generation's first revival. And social media connected Christians and soon-to-be Christians to these kids and their story and their God in a way that wasn't possible just decades before.

Just as in the 1960s and 1970s, the youngest generations of Americans were hurting. We felt lonely, isolated, ignored, scared, and desperate for change. We were looking for something—anything—we could hold on to and believe in. And out of all of the options available to them, the students at Asbury University chose God.

The events in early 2023 led to thousands and thousands of baptisms, just like the events half a century before. And every time the spirit of a people changes, so does their heart for society around them. Spiritual revival always leads to social renewal because the heart of God is good, and He "causes his sun to rise on the evil and the good, and sends rain on the righteous and the unrighteous" (Matthew 5:45). This is the heavenly work of Christians on earth, to extend the inviting grace of God to everyone around us.

Your family and friends, your neighbors and enemies, all genuinely want something better. They all agree that something is wrong. They all want the pain and suffering to go away. But once again, the difference is in the solution.

Progressives want to fix what is wrong by running as far away from America and God as they can. Conservatives want to fix what is wrong by restoring the shine of America, the beacon of hope for the world. And the conservatives who are also Christians—well, they know the only way for America to be America once again is through spiritual revival by the grace of God.

We can learn a lot from the way members of my generation went about seeking change: Those changed by the revival sought God—the answer to all their hopes and dreams— through prayer. After a tumultuous three years of death and destruction in the country, Millennials and Gen Z showed their fellow Americans the path to the only stable place they knew: the presence of God. We would all do well to follow in their footsteps.

We Christians, as a people, are subject to God. We must lead America on the way back to the favor of the Lord through prayer. And we must serve God and our neighbors in love and truth. We must be the ones who first celebrate the truth that "It is for freedom that Christ has set us free" and that we should continue to lead the way for ourselves, our families, our friends, and our fellow citizens in standing firm so that we "do not let yourselves be burdened again by a yoke of slavery" (Galatians 5:1).

This was the mindset of the pilgrims when they left Europe to build a shining city on the hill. This was surely in the thinking of the Founders when they called upon God to help them create a new nation, securing life, liberty, and happiness for all. It was assuredly the hope of the brave men and women who fought against the evolutionist and communist ideology that destroyed humans to save humanity during the world wars. And if we want any shot at continuing this great American experiment, we must continue the long-standing faith of praying for continued freedom.

Here Comes the Queen

The story of Esther, from the Bible, is about courage and divine purpose. If it has been a while since you have read or listened to the story, I'll refresh your memory!

Esther, a Jewish orphan raised by her cousin Mordecai, found herself in a crazy situation when she was chosen through a royal beauty contest to become the Queen of Persia.

Out of hatred for all Jews (but not directly related to Esther's new role), a man named Haman, who served as an advisor to the King, devised a plan to murder all of the Jewish people in Persia.

Mordecai, realizing the gravity of the situation, urged Queen Esther to use her position to intercede with King

Xerxes, reveal her Jewish heritage, and thwart Haman's evil plot.

Esther initially hesitated, as approaching the king without being requested by him could result in her execution. This would take guts. This could end more than just her career; it could easily end her life.

Mordecai reminded her that she might have been placed in her position "for such a time as this."

Esther listened to Mordecai's inspiring advice and decided to take the risk and save the lives of the entire Jewish population. Esther's bravery paid off as she found favor with the king, who spared her life and listened to her plea. She revealed Haman's wicked plan, which ultimately led to Haman's downfall and the salvation of the Jewish people.

Over the years, the phrase "for such a time as this" has become a symbol of recognizing one's unique calling and destiny, even in the face of danger and adversity, as Esther did to save her people. This story highlights the idea that God puts people in certain positions or circumstances for a specific purpose, and they must rise to the occasion when the moment demands it.

We are in such a moment right now. This is it. God put us all here today together "for such a time as this." God does not make mistakes. This is not a coincidence. I believe that we, the intersection of all freedom-loving people from across every generation and part of God's meticulously planned-out strategy, can set America back on track.

And, I must say, my generation is in a position to bring revival to the nation. My generation is prepared for such a time as this to save America.

In the second chapter of this book, I told the story of a lady who approached me after a speech, apologizing on behalf of her generation for leaving us with this mess. I find myself in a very similar conversation just about every day. It's not their fault. It really isn't. This isn't one generation, one person, or one party's fault. But I feel strongly that if the older and wiser generations among us don't help Gen Z step up right now to fight for America, there will be plenty of blame to go around. The carnage of the failed experiment will be on our hands. This is our last shot to save the shining city on the hill.

> *My generation is prepared for such a time as this to save America.*

Unlike many in the mainstream media, I don't make a living as a fearmonger. I never wanted this book to scare any of you but to prepare you, much like Ronald Reagan prepared the American people to fight for what is good and right.

This book got its name from a Reagan quote. The pages you just read were filled with timeless words of wisdom from the fortieth president. I think it's only appropriate if I close the book with a final quote attributed to Ronald Reagan that encompasses the whole mission of this book: "History comes and history goes, but principles endure, and ensure future generations will defend liberty not as a gift from government but as a blessing from our Creator."

We have a responsibility to ensure the principles this great nation was founded upon endure. We have a responsibility to continue to be that "shining city on a hill." We have a responsibility to be that instantly recognizable land of freedom. The words "freedom" and "America" should be synonymous.

To accomplish that, we cannot betray our past and the many generations of brave Americans who battled against the enemies of America, both foreign and domestic. We can't squander our freedom by sitting by and doing nothing, hoping that the powers that seek to undermine America will stop their attack. There is much to be done, and I invite you to join me at the table to do the work.

The time is now because we've all been made for "such a time as this."

Step up, be bold, speak out. We've got a country to save.

EPILOGUE

This journey began on September 17, 2023 (which happens to be Constitution Day).

I was sitting in church, and the guest preacher that day wasn't really grabbing my attention. I had spent the previous week speaking at a college campus about the importance of my generation stepping up right now in American history to save our country. I wanted that message to get out to more people, but I didn't know how. I started praying. Right then, right there, in the middle of the service, I asked God what I could do to amplify this message.

I flipped over the bulletin from that Sunday and on the back, wrote out a bare-bones outline of the book that you just finished reading.

That afternoon, I texted a dear friend who was a published author and told her that I needed to speak to her tomorrow about an urgent idea. She could have easily waved me off, but she set up a time, and I shared with her the idea the next day.

The next Monday, I was out of school, and we met at a local coffee shop. For eight hours, I sat on my laptop and typed out the proposal for this book. She spent her entire day offering suggestions, giving guidance on how to put together something to be considered by publishers, and sharing her own experiences. She congratulated me on accomplishing the first step and told me to be patient as it takes a few weeks and even sometimes a few months to hear back from publishers.

The next morning, before going to school, I emailed the proposal for *One Generation Away* to every publisher I could think of. By the time I got home from school, I already had six responses.

I was overwhelmed. I fired off a text to a spiritual mentor of mine asking for prayers and guidance. He gave me both and then offered something else; he sent me the number of a literary agent. He was used by a mutual friend of ours, for whom I had great respect. I texted him that night and signed him on to my team within the next twenty-four hours.

I started writing this book in the middle of October with the goal of getting it out in time for the 2024 election. This manuscript was due in the middle of December. I had roughly two months to write the book you are reading, and I couldn't be prouder of the way it turned out. The truth is, I'm a writer at heart. I always have been, and I always will be. I started *The Truth Gazette* by writing weekly articles. Today, I still write articles, but I also write podcast scripts, interview questions, and tweets. I've dreamed of writing a book one day; I just never ever imagined that "one day" would come while I was still in high school.

The point of my sharing this whole behind-the-scenes story with you was this: I did not write this book alone, nor could I have. This book was solely possible by the power and grace of God. He set everything up to work out perfectly. He connected me with the right people at the right time. He was the one who got me through the hard times when I thought this project would never make it to the finish line. When I was told time and time again that it was impossible for a seventeen-year-old to write a book by himself and publish it by the age of eighteen, He believed in me and walked with me every step of the way. He is the reason you were able to read this book, so before I thank anybody else, I first have to thank Him.

Thank you, God, for making this dream a reality. Thank you for walking with me through this process and guiding me the whole way. Thank you for giving me the unique opportunity to hopefully inspire the next generation. Thank you for letting me grow more during this two-month writing process than I have in my entire time on Earth. Thank you!

If you've made it this far, before you close this book, let me offer you one piece of advice: When I began this book, everybody said an eighteen-year-old could not write his own book without a ghost writer. Then, when I proved them wrong, they said I could not get my book published. Well, here we are. My whole career, people have told me that it wasn't possible and that I needed to "wait my turn." I hope those same people see this book at their local bookstore and pick it up in shock.

Never give up. Never listen to those who say it's "not your time." Through Christ, you are stronger than you know. As you close this book and move forward in life, take these four call-to-actions with you:

Change the world. Prove them wrong. Save America. Glorify the Lord.

Acknowledgments

I start by thanking my mom and my dad. I remember the night I came into your room before bedtime with this idea. You believed in me and the mission of this book but knew how difficult writing a book in two months while also being a junior in high school would be—but you supported me, nonetheless. I could not have stayed strong enough to put this whole thing together if it were not for your constant love and support, not just during this project but over the last seven years of my abnormal teenage political career. You have canceled plans, taken off of work, woken up early, and stayed out late, traveling the country with me to make this all possible. Thank you. Thank you. Thank you. I love you both so much, and I hope I can be half the parents y'all have been for me to my kids one day.

To Ainslee, my sister: Thank you for helping me keep this book a secret while I wrote it. Thank you for not revealing it at the lunch table at school, and thank you for always coming in to check on me after long days of writing. I love you!

To Granny and Paw Paw: Thank you for everything. Thank you for always supporting me. Thank you for always letting me come over and hang out. Thank you for always being willing to talk politics with me or bake cookies or brownies for me. I'll always remember the day, right before I finished the manuscript, when I finally told you about the book. The excitement on your faces made this worth it. I love you both so much!

To Papa Doug: Thank you for helping me get my start. My weekly articles would have never turned into *The Truth Gazette* if it wasn't for you always forwarding my articles to all of your friends. They would sign up for my emails and then tell their friends, and here we are today. And you didn't just stop there. You have supported me every step of the way, driven to countless events with me, and given me hundreds of nuggets of wisdom and encouraging advice. I love you so much, and I wish Nana was here to celebrate this book with us in person!

To Nana: Thank you for being the greatest guardian angel of all time! I hope I'm making you proud! I love you so much!

To my entire extended family: Thank you. Thank you for putting up with my craziness, thank you for working around my schedule for family events, and thank you for loving and supporting me regardless of the situation. This book would not have been possible without each and every one of you pouring into my life, and I love you all so much!

To my friends: I truly am so incredibly blessed. God surrounded me with the best support circle possible, and I could not thank him enough for all of you. Thank you all for sticking with me, even when times have gotten tough. Thank you for still letting me be a normal teenager. Thank you for bearing with me and supporting me through this whole journey. Thank you for ignoring the haters who have DMed you all and threatened you for being friends with me. Thank you for everything! Maybe now I can have a little bit more time to play golf or go to cookout now that I'm done writing!

To my "kitchen cabinet" of advisors: You know who you are! You're the lifelong friends I lean on when I'm struggling. You're the same lifelong friends there to celebrate with me after a big accomplishment. You're the mentors I've looked up to and turned to countless times. You're the first people I text about anything and everything. Thank you. Thank you for being there for me no matter what. I'm always here if I can repay the favor!

To my prayer warriors: Thank you for being the only people who knew about this book during the writing period who I turned to when things looked impossible. Thank you for standing alongside me and being there for me this entire time. Thank you for not blocking my number after countless prayer request texts. I hope I can be there for all of you like you were there for me. I love you all!

To my school administrators and teachers: Thank you for making this possible. Thank you for allowing me to get this book done and still get an education at the same time. Thank you to all of the teachers and admins, former and current, who have supported me along the way. I hope I can make you all proud! Go Knights!

To my church and youth group: Thank you for the prayers and support during this entire process. I hope this book can start a revival to glorify God!

To Jody and Dr. McKee: Thank you for leading me to make the best decision of my life—accepting Christ.

To Ginger: Thank you for making this book a reality. Thank you for the wisdom and coaching to take this book from a scribbled-out plan to a hardcover on a shelf!

To Katie and Wesley Britt: Thank you for your constant support and checking in during this entire process. I've been blessed to meet and work with a lot of people in the movement, but none have become true, genuine friends like both of you! Thank you for believing in me and being my biggest cheerleaders this whole time!

To the Republican National Committee: Thank you for reading my January 2023 op-ed and trusting me enough to let me found and co-chair the inaugural Youth Advisory Council. Thank you for putting up with my new ideas and not just putting them in a comment box but making them happen in real life. Thank you for giving my generation a seat at the table, and not just the kid's table. Let this book be another nail in the coffin of the Democrats' past monopoly on my generation!

To my RNC co-chair, CJ Pearson: Thank you for answering my call to put the whole idea of a youth council together. Thank you for believing in my idea enough to see its potential. We made history at the RNC, and I couldn't have done it without you! I hope you enjoy this book!

To Marcus Costantino: Thank you for seeing the vision and making it a reality. Thank you for letting this be entirely my book with entirely my ideas and passion but being there to offer advice and coaching on how to successfully and effectively get my points across. I have never enjoyed Zoom calls as much as I did during the writing of this book! Thank you for sticking with me even when you could have run the other way and for not making fun of me for being a history nerd. You have to come down for a Bama game at some point!

To Tom Dean: Thank you. Thank you for being the best mentor and literary agent I could have ever asked for. Thank you for taking my proposal and putting it in front of the right people. Thank you for believing in me and not running away when times got tough. Thank you for your patience, guidance, wisdom, and, most importantly, thank you for seeing the potential in this book when everybody else said a teenager couldn't do it. Thank you, Tom! You are truly the best! If I got anything out of this, it was a new friend! Roll Tide!

To Kathryn Riggs and the entire Regnery and Skyhorse publishing team: Thank you for believing in me to write this book. Thank you for trusting me during the entire process and guiding me every step of the way. From our first call, I knew that you were more like family than colleagues, and that remains true today. You took a chance on me, and I hope I made you all proud! Thank you for everything!

To everyone who has supported me since I began this journey at the age of eleven: Thank you. You all truly are the reason I still am here today. Thank you for supporting me, thank you for encouraging me, and thank you for believing in me. I hope you continue to stand alongside me for years to come, and that this is one of many books you get to read and enjoy.

APPENDIX A
Next Steps for My Peers

I urge, then, first of all, that petitions, prayers, intercession and thanksgiving be made for all people—for kings and all those in authority, that we may live peaceful and quiet lives in all godliness and holiness. This is good, and pleases God our Savior, who wants all people to be saved and to come to a knowledge of the truth.
—1 TIMOTHY 2:1–2

I constantly get messages from people across the country asking how to get involved or just simply what they can do to get started! I thought this was a perfect opportunity to share a quick crash course of next steps after reading this book on how to now actually save America. Here they are:

1. Pray
Study what God says about being a Christian in the world in
which we live.

Start with 1 Timothy 2:1–4, Hosea 8:4, Proverbs 28:12,
Acts 5:27–29, Romans 13:1–7, 1 Samuel 12:13–25, and
Proverbs 14:34.

2. Learn
See the *Suggested Resources* in Appendix B and get started
watching and reading. Read as much as you can and then
write as much as you can. (Tweets don't count.)

3. Vote!
Your vote really does matter. Stop venting. Join the process. Start solving problems. Emphasize to your peers the
importance of voting. Share with them that their vote really
does matter, too! Tell them about Christopher Poulson in
Connecticut who won by only one vote.

4. Be Persistent and Resilient
Never, ever, ever give up. Always keep trying. Prove the people wrong who told you you're too young or that it wasn't
possible. They are naysayers, and there are more than enough
of them in the world. Tune them out and be a positive force
for change.

5. Get Involved Where God Is Already at Work
Join any conservative chapter or organization you can find—
just get plugged in. There is strength in numbers and working

alongside your peers as opposed to against them is way more effective!

Speak out. Serve at a local pregnancy center. Start a Bible study. Send emails to your elected officials. Share a conservative post to story. Do something! Anything! It's time to get up off the sidelines!

APPENDIX B
Suggested Resources

My Trusted Sources

Prager University	www.prageru.com
Hillsdale College	www.hillsdale.edu
Ronald Reagan Presidential Library	www.reaganlibrary.gov
Khan Academy	www.khanacademy.org
The Story of America	www.thestoryofamerica.us
Got Questions	www.gotquestions.org
The Bible Project	www.bibleproject.com

My Current and Future Reading List

Thank You for Arguing: What Aristotle, Lincoln, and Homer Simpson Can Teach Us about the Art of Persuasion (Jay Heinrichs)

The Ruthless Elimination of Hurry: How to Stay Emotionally Healthy and Spiritually Alive in the Chaos of the Modern World (John Mark Comer)

American Marxism (Mark Levin)

If You Can Keep It: The Forgotten Promise of American Liberty (Eric Metaxas)

Never Enough: A Navy Seal Commander on Living a Life of Excellence, Agility, and Meaning (Mike Hayes)

When Character Was King: A Story of Ronald Reagan (Peggy Noonan)

Politics for People Who Hate Politics: How to Engage Without Losing Your Friends or Selling Your Soul (Denise Grace Gitsham)

10 Books That Screwed Up the World: And 5 Others That Didn't Help (Benjamin Wiker)

Worshipping the State: How Liberalism Became Our State Religion (Benjamin Wiker)

America: The Last Best Hope (Volumes I, II, and III), (William J. Bennett)

1984 (George Orwell)

Animal Farm (George Orwell)

The Politics Industry, How Political Innovation Can Break Partisan Gridlock and Save Our Democracy (Katherine M. Gehl and Michael E. Porter)

The Patriot's Reference: Documents, Speeches and Sermons That Compose the American Soul (Joel J. Miller and Kristen Parrish)

Eraced: Uncovering the Lies of Critical Race Theory and Abortion (John K. Amanchukwu Sr.)

America: To Pray? Or Not to Pray? (David Barton)

About the Author

Brilyn Hollyhand is an eighteen-year-old political commentator and strategist who has captured the attention of the nation with his astute observations and unique perspective. As founder and editor-in-chief of *The Truth Gazette*, a conservative news service he established at the age of eleven, Brilyn has proven himself to be a force to be reckoned with in the world of politics.

Despite his youth, he does not lack experience. Brilyn has already interviewed an impressive array of influential figures for his podcast, *The Brilyn Hollyhand Show. The Brilyn Hollyhand Show* is available on major podcast platforms including YouTube, Spotify, Apple Podcasts, iHeart, and anywhere else you watch or listen to podcasts.

Brilyn makes regular appearances on national cable news networks to give his unique perspective on the news of the day.

Brilyn has harnessed social media to build a distinct brand and get his message out directly to his generation. He has had several uber-viral videos over the years, reaching an audience of millions across numerous platforms. You can follow Brilyn on all major social media apps with the handle @BrilynHollyhand.

In 2022, Brilyn's dedication and accomplishments earned him the prestigious John Lewis National Youth Leadership Award from the National Secretaries of State Association. This distinguished recognition celebrated his outstanding contributions to politics at such a young age, highlighting his immense potential and promising future.

At the beginning of 2023, Brilyn was appointed to co-chair the RNC's inaugural Youth Advisory Council. He has interviewed and offered advice on how to win the youth vote to President Donald J. Trump several times, as well as 2024 presidential candidates Ron DeSantis, Nikki Haley, Tim Scott, Mike Pence, Vivek Ramaswamy, and Robert F. Kennedy Jr. His op-eds on youth engagement in politics have appeared in TownHall, Human Events, and The Post Millennial; his long-form article from January of 2023, calling his party out for their lack of focus on his generation, received national attention.

One Generation Away is Brilyn Hollyhand's debut book, published at the age of eighteen.

Follow Brilyn: **@BrilynHollyhand** on Facebook, Twitter, Instagram, TikTok, and YouTube.

ENDNOTES

Introduction

1 Ronald Reagan, "Inaugural Address (Public Ceremony)," Ronald Reagan Presidential Library & Museum, January 5, 1967, https://www.reaganlibrary.gov/archives/speech/january-5–1967-inaugural-address-public-ceremony, emphasis added.

2 Ibid., emphasis added.

3 Ibid.

4 Ibid.

5 Ronald Reagan, "Inaugural Address 1981," Ronald Reagan Presidential Library & Museum, January 20, 1981, https://www.reaganlibrary.gov/archives/speech/inaugural-address-1981#:~:text=It%20is%20time%20for%20us,us%20if%20we%20do%20nothing.

6 Joe Concha, "Education Blunder Igniting Suburban Parents Driving McAuliffe Panic in Virginia," *The Hill*, October 28, 2021, https://thehill.com/opinion/campaign/578885-education-blunder-igniting-suburban-parents-driving-mcauliffe-panic-in/.

7 Ronald Reagan, "A Time for Choosing Speech," Ronald Reagan Presidential Library & Museum, October 27, 1964, https://www.reaganlibrary.gov/archives/speech/time-choosing-speech.

Chapter 1

1 Ecclesiastes 1:9.

2 Google Books Ngram Viewer, "teenager," https://books.google.com/ngrams/graph?content=teenager&year_start=1800&year_end=2019&corpus=en-2019&smoothing=3, last accessed December 29, 2023.

3   Saumya Joseph, "Depression, Anxiety Rising among U.S. College Students," Reuters, August 29, 2019, https://www.reuters.com/article /us-health-mental-undergrads-idUSKCN1VJ25Z/.

4   Dennis Prager, "Why Are So Many Young People Unhappy," PragerU, March 2, 2020, https://www.prageru.com/video/why-are -so-many-young-people-unhappy Time 55s-1.14s.

5   Frank Newport, "Percentage of Christians in U.S. Drifting Down, but Still High," Gallup, December 24, 2015, https://www.govinfo.gov /content/pkg/USCOURTS-ca4–15-02597/pdf/USCOURTS-ca4 –15-02597–3.pdf.

6   Gregory Smith, "About Three-in-Ten U.S. Adults Are Now Religiously Unaffiliated," Pew Research Center, December 14, 2021, https: //www.pewresearch.org/religion/2021/12/14/about-three-in-ten -u-s-adults-are-now-religiously-unaffiliated/.

7   The Firm for Men, "How Marriage & Divorce Have Changed Since the 1950s," https://www.thefirmformen.com/articles/how-marriage -divorce-have-changed-since-the-1950s/#:~:text=While%20the%20 marriage%20rate%20in,1958%20divorce%20rate%20was%20 2.1, last accessed on December 28, 2023.

8   Petrelli Previtera, "Divorce Statistics for 2022," https://www.petrel lilaw.com/divorce-statistics-for-2022/#:~:text=What%20is%20 the%20Current%20Divorce,to%20the%20U.S.%20Census%20 Bureau, last accessed on December 28, 2023.

9   Joanne Beckman, "Religion in Post-World War II America," National Humanities Center, https://nationalhumanitiescenter.org /tserve/twenty/tkeyinfo/trelww2.htm.

10   The Cigna Group, "The Loneliness Epidemic Persists: A Post-Pandemic Look at the State of Loneliness among U.S. Adults," https://newsroom.thecignagroup.com/loneliness-epidemic-persists -post-pandemic-look, last accessed on December 29, 2023.

11   Ronald Reagan, "Labor Day Speech at Liberty State Park, Jersey City, New Jersey," Ronald Reagan Presidential Library & Museum, September 1, 1980, https://www.reaganlibrary.gov/archives/speech /labor-day-speech-liberty-state-park-jersey-city-new-jersey.

Chapter 2

1   "Marxism," *Oxford Learner's Dictionaries*, https://www.oxford learnersdictionaries.com/us/definition/english/marxism?q=marxism.

2   "Communism," Oxford Learner's Dictionaries, https://www.oxford learnersdictionaries.com/us/definition/english/communism ?q=communism.

3   "Socialism," *Oxford Learner's Dictionaries*, https://www.oxford learnersdictionaries.com/us/definition/english/socialism?q=socialism.

4   Saul Alinsky, *Rules for Radicals: A Pragmatic Primer for Realistic Radicals* (New York: Random House, Inc., 1971, book edition 1989), Chapter 7, Kindle.

5   Binyamin Appelbaum and Jim Tankersley, "What Could Kill Booming U.S. Economy? 'Socialists.' White House Warns," *New York Times*, October 23, 2018, https://www.nytimes.com/2018/10/23/us/politics /socialist-democrats-trump-elections.html.

6   Summit Ministries "desires to see generations of Christians mobilized to transform a broken world." They "exist to equip and support rising generations to embrace God's truth and champion a biblical worldview." See www.summit.org.

7   Jeff Myers, "What Is Marxism? A Five-Minute Primer," *The Western Journal*, July 15, 2020, https://www.westernjournal.com /jeff-myers-marxism-five-minute-primer/.

8   Vladimir Lenin, *The State and Revolution*, in Lenin, *Essential Works of Lenin* (New York, NY: Dover, 1987), Chapter I, Section I, 272.

9   "Third All-Russia Congress of Soviets of Workers', Soldiers' and Peasants' Deputies." *Pravda* Nos. 9, 10 ,and 15, January 26–27 and February 02, 1918. Collected Works, Volume 26, 459–461.

10 Phil Magness, "Why Universities Have Shifted to the Political Left in the past 20 Years," Areo, July 12, 2017, https://areomagazine. com/2017/12/07/why-universities-have-shifted-to-the-political-left -in-the-past-20-years/.

11 Ibid.

12 Dr. Stephen Flick, "The Christian Founding of Harvard," Christian Heritage Foundation, September 8, 2023, https://christianheritag efellowship.com/the-christian-founding-of-harvard/.

13 Benjamin Wiker, *Ten Books That Screwed Up the World: And 5 Others That Didn't Help* (Washington, DC: Regnery, 2008), 70–71.

14 Valerie Strauss, "How Harvard, Penn, MIT Leaders Answered—or Skirted—Questions on Antisemitism," *Washington Post*, December 6, 2023, https://www.washingtonpost.com/education/2023/12/06/3-elite -college-presidents-answered-questions-antisemitism/.

15 "ICYMI: Stefanik Demands Answers from Harvard President Claudine Gay on Harvard's Failure to Condemn Antisemitism and Anti-Israel Attacks on Campus," Elise Stefanik, December 5, 2023, https://stefanik.house.gov/2023/12/icymi-stefanik-demands-answers -from-harvard-president-claudine-gay-on-harvard-s-failure-to -condemn-antisemitism-and-anti-israel-attacks-on-campus.

16 Dennis Prager, "Young Americans Are Not Taught About Evil," American Greatness, August 29, 2023, https://amgreatness.com/2023 /08/29/young-americans-are-not-taught-about-evil/.

17 Ronald Reagan, "Tear Down This Wall!," delivered July 17, 1980, National Center for Public Policy, November 4, 2001, https://nationalcenter.org/ncppr/2001/11/04/ronald-reagans-berlin-tear-down-this-wall-speech-1987/.
18 Ronald Reagan, "A Time for Choosing Speech," Ronald Reagan Presidential Library & Museum, October 27, 1964, https://www.reaganlibrary.gov/archives/speech/time-choosing-speech.
19 Ronald Reagan, "Remarks at the Annual Convention of the National Association of Evangelicals in Orlando, FL," Ronald Reagan Presidential Library & Museum, March 8, 1983, https://www.reaganlibrary.gov/archives/speech/remarks-annual-convention-national-association-evangelicals-orlando-fl.

Chapter 3
1 HBO, *The Newsroom*, Season 2, Episode 4.
2 Ibid.
3 This popular quote from Mark Twain is the title of a book: *Man Is the Only Animal That Blushes . . . or Needs To: The Wisdom of Mark Twain*, published by Stanyan Books and Random House in 1971.
4 Ronald Reagan, "Inaugural Address (Public Ceremony)," Ronald Reagan Presidential Library & Museum, January 5, 1967, https://www.reaganlibrary.gov/archives/speech/january-5–1967-inaugural-address-public-ceremony.
5 "Why Elvis Presley Was Censored on *The Ed Sullivan Show*," elvisbiography.net, revised October 28, 2020, https://elvisbiography.net/2020/09/09/why-elvis-presley-was-censored-on-the-ed-sullivan-show/.
6 Gary Trust, "Cardi B & Megan Thee Stallion's 'WAP' Debuts at No. 1 on Billboard Hot 100 With Record First-Week Streams," Billboard, August 17, 2020, https://www.billboard.com/pro/cardi-bs-wap-debuts-no-1-hot-100/.

Chapter 4
1 Josh Katz, "Who Will Be President?" *New York Times*, November 8, 2016, https://www.nytimes.com/interactive/2016/upshot/presidential-polls-forecast.html.
2 John Podesta Statement on Election-Night Results, "Road to the White House 2016," CSPAN, November 9, 2016, https://www.c-span.org/video/?418089–1/john-podesta-statement-election-night-results.
3 Ciara McCarthy and Claire Phipps, "US Election 2016 Results Timeline: How the Night Unfolded," *Guardian*, November 9, 2016, https://www.theguardian.com/us-news/2016/nov/08/presidential-election-updates-trump-clinton-news.

4 Jennifer Rubin, "Trump's America Is a Rotten Place," *Washington Post*, January 20, 2017, https://www.washingtonpost.com/blogs/right-turn/wp/2017/01/20/trumps-america-is-a-rotten-place/.

5 Charles Blow, "Trump and the Parasitic Presidency," *New York Times*, March 13, 2017, https://www.nytimes.com/2017/03/13/opinion/trump-and-the-parasitic-presidency.html.

6 Rich Lowry, "Trump the Troll," *Politico Magazine*, May 24, 2017, https://www.politico.com/magazine/story/2017/05/24/trump-the-troll-215188/.

7 Thomas E. Patterson, "News Coverage of Donald Trump's First 100 Days," Harvard Kennedy School, May 28, 2017, https://shorenstein center.org/news-coverage-donald-trumps-first-100-days/.

8 Ibid.

9 Ibid.

10 George Bernard Shaw, https://www.azquotes.com/quote/1231941.

11 Emma-Jo Morris and Gabrielle Fonrouge, "Smoking-Gun Email Reveals How Hunter Biden Introduced Ukrainian Businessman to VP Dad," *New York Post*, October 14, 2020, https://nypost.com/2020/10/14/email-reveals-how-hunter-biden-introduced-ukrainian-biz-man-to-dad/.

12 Zachary Cohen, Devan Cole, Tierney Sneed, Evan Perez, Hannah Rabinowitz, Jeremy Herb, and Marshall Cohen, "Special Counsel John Durham Concludes FBI Never Should Have Launched Full Trump-Russia Probe," CNN, May 16, 2023, https://www.cnn.com/2023/05/15/politics/john-durham-report-fbi-trump-released/index.html.

13 Aaron Smith, "The Internet's Role in Campaign 2008," Pew Research Center, April 15, 2009, https://www.pewresearch.org/internet/2009/04/15/the-internets-role-in-campaign-2008/.

14 Thomas G. Del Beccaro, "America's Tradition of Media Bias," *Washington Times*, October 18, 2016, https://www.washingtontimes.com/news/2016/oct/18/americas-tradition-of-media-bias.

15 Ibid.

16 Ibid.

17 Ibid.

18 Joe Concha, "Journalism Is Now Opinion-Based—Not News-Based," *The Hill*, May 24, 2019, https://thehill.com/opinion/white-house/445385-journalism-is-now-opinion-based-not-news-based/.

19 "U.S. Journalism Has Become More Subjective," Rand Corporation, May 14, 2019, https://www.rand.org/news/press/2019/05/14.html.

20 Concha, "Journalism Is Now Opinion-Based—Not News-Based."

21 Megan Brenan, "Americans' Trust in Media Remains Near Record Low," Gallup, October 18, 2022, https://news.gallup.com/poll/403166/americans-trust-media-remains-near-record-low.aspx.
22 Ibid.
23 Ibid.
24 " Winning the Media Campaign: How the Press Reported the 2008 General Election," Pew Research, October 22, 2008, https://www.pewresearch.org/journalism/2008/10/22/winning-media-campaign/.
25 Thomas E. Patterson, "News Coverage of the 2016 General Election: How the Press Failed the Voters," Harvard Kennedy School Shorenstein Center on Media, Politics and Public Policy, December 7, 2016, https://shorensteincenter.org/news-coverage-2016-general-election/.
26 George Bernard Shaw, https://www.azquotes.com/quote/1231941.
27 Ronald Reagan, "Republican National Convention Acceptance Speech, 1980," Ronald Reagan Presidential Library & Museum, July 17, 1980, https://www.reaganlibrary.gov/archives/speech/republican-national-convention-acceptance-speech-1980.
28 Ronald Reagan, "To Restore America," Ronald Reagan Presidential Library & Museum,https://www.reaganlibrary.gov/archives/speech/restore-america.

Chapter 5
1 G. K. Chesterton, "What I Saw in America" https://www.chesterton.org/america/.
2 "Creed," *Merriam-Webster Dictionary*,https://www.merriam-webster.com/dictionary/creed.
3 "Religion and Congregations in a Time of Social and Political Upheaval," Public Religion Research Institute, May 5, 2023, https://www.prri.org/research/religion-and-congregations-in-a-time-of-social-and-political-upheaval/.
4 "John Adams on Religion and the Constitution" Liberty Fund, Inc., https://oll.libertyfund.org/quote/john-adams-religion-constitution.
5 David Barton, *America: To Pray? Or Not to Pray?* (Aledo, Texas: WallBuilder Press, 1995), 29.
6 Ibid., see chart on page 40.
7 Ibid., see chart on page 53.
8 Ibid., see chart on page 58.
9 Ibid., 76.
10 Benjamin Wiker, *Worshipping the State: How Liberalism Became Our State Religion,* (Washington, DC: Regnery, 2013).
11 Ibid., 123.

12 Daniel A. Cox, "Generation Z and the Future of Faith in America," Survey Center on American Life, March 24, 2022, https://www .americansurveycenter.org/research/generation-z-future-of-faith/.

13 Katrin Trinko, "Gen Z Is the Loneliest Generation, and It's Not Just Because of Social Media: The Loneliness of Generation Z Reflects Not Just Rising Social Media Use but a Broader Decline in Interactions with Neighbors, Co-workers and Church Friends," *USA Today*, May 3, 2018, https://www.usatoday.com /story/opinion/2018/05/03/gen-z-loneliest-generation-social -media-personal-interactions-column/574701002/.

14 C. S. Lewis, *Mere Christianity* (San Francisco, CA: HarperSanFrancisco, Harper edition, 2001), 134.

15 This is a list of the fruit of the Spirit in Galatians 5:22–23.

Chapter 6

1   Diane Werts, "Why We Need Our Slice of Mayberry," CNN, July 4, 2012, https://www.cnn.com/2012/07/03/opinion/werts-andy-griffith /index.html.

2   This is one of four oil paintings made by Norman Rockwell capturing the spirit of Franklin D. Roosevelt's 1941 State of the Union address. The four paintings are titled: *Freedom of Speech*, *Freedom of Worship*, *Freedom from Want*, and *Freedom from Fear*. See https: //en.wikipedia.org/wiki/Four_Freedoms_(Rockwell).

3   Melissa S. Kearney, "The Explosive Rise of Single-Parent Families Is Not a Good Thing," *New York Times*, September 17, 2023, https: //www.nytimes.com/2023/09/17/opinion/single-parent-families -income-inequality-college.html.

4   Pew Research Center, "The Future of the Family," September 14, 2023, https://www.pewresearch.org/social-trends/2023/09/14/the-future -of-the-family/.

5   Bob Yirka, "Study Suggests Larger Families Have More Conservative Views," phys.org, March 24, 2020, https://phys.org/news/2020–03 -larger-families-views.html.

6   Webroot, "Internet Pornorahy by the Numbers; A Significant Threat to Society," https://www.webroot.com/us/en/resources/tips-arti-cles/internet-pornography-by-the-numbers#:~:text=About%20 200%2C000%20Americans%20are%20classified,downloads%20 are%20related%20to%20pornography (last accessed on December 31, 2023).

Chapter 7

1   Aimee Picchi, "Twitter Files: What They Are and Why They Matter," CBS News, December 14, 2022, https://www.cbsnews.com/news /twitter-files-matt-taibbi-bari-weiss-michael-shellenberger-elon-musk/.

2 Alexandra Marquez, "Poll: Gun Ownership Reaches Record High with American Electorate," NBC News, November 21, 2023, https://www.nbcnews.com/meet-the-press/meetthepressblog/poll-gun-ownership-reaches-record-high-american-electorate-rcna126037.

3 "Republic," *American Heritage Dictionary of the English Language*, https://ahdictionary.com/word/search.html?q=republic.

4 Zachary S. Elkins, "Underestimated but Undeterred: The 27th Amendment and the Power of Tenacious Citizenship," Cambridge Core, August 11, 2022, https://www.cambridge.org/core/journals/ps-political-science-and-politics/article/underestimated-but-undeterred-the-27th-amendment-and-the-power-of-tenacious-citizenship/1912F2DC90242C6A484D340B83437E4B.

5 Ronald Reagan, "Farewell Address to the Nation, January 11, 1989," Ronald Reagan Presidential Library & Museum, https://www.reaganlibrary.gov/archives/speech/farewell-address-nation, accessed November 25, 2023.

6 Aaron Zitner, "Voters See American Dream Slipping Out of Reach, WSJ/NORC Poll Shows," *Wall Street Journal*, November 24, 2023, https://www.wsj.com/us-news/american-dream-out-of-reach-poll-3b774892?.

7 "American Dream Has Turned Elusive, Voters Say," *Wall Street Journal*, November 24, 2023, https://www.wsj.com/us-news/american-dream-out-of-reach-poll-3b774892?mod=article_inline.

8 Ronald Reagan, *An American Life* (New York, NY: Simon & Schuster, 1990), 28.

Chapter 8

1 "Courage," Dictionary.com, https://www.dictionary.com/browse/courage.

2 Edison Research, "Youth Prefer Democrats by 28-Point Margin," Tisch College, last accessed on December 14, 2023, https://circle.tufts.edu/2022-election-center#youth-prefer-democrats-by-28-point-margin.

3 Ibid.

4 Ibid.

5 Ibid.

6 Katherine Schaeffer, "The Changing Faces of Congress in 8 Charts," Pew Research Center, February 7, 2023, https://www.pewresearch.org/short-reads/2023/02/07/the-changing-face-of-congress/#:~:text=The%20118th%20Congress%20is%20the,and%2012%25%20of%20the%20Senate.

7 House Judiciary Committee, "US House Judiciary Republicans: DOJ Labeled Dozens of Parents as Terrorist Threats," May 20, 2022,

https://judiciary.house.gov/media/press-releases/us-house-judiciary-republicans-doj-labeled-dozens-of-parents-as-terrorist.

8   Shannon Thaler, "Bud Light Parent Anheuser-Busch's Stock Has Lost $27B over Dylan Mulvaney," *New York Post*, June 2, 2023, https://nypost.com/2023/06/02/bud-light-parent-anheuser-buschs-stock-lost-27b-over-dylan-mulvaney/.

9   "Georgia Senate Runoff Results," PBS, https://www.pbs.org/newshour/elections-2020/georgia-senate-runoff.

10 Annie McCormick and Bob Brooks, "Nearly 1.5 Million Pennsylvanians Have Already Cast Ballots Ahead of Election," ABC 6, October 24, 2020, https://6abc.com/vote-pa-2020-election-mail-in-ballot-voting-pennsylvania/7283354/.

Chapter 9

1   Ron Grossman, "Flashback: A Crisis of Conscience over Slavery Gave Birth to a Formidable Political Force: The Republican Party," *Chicago Tribune*, February 26, 2021, https://www.chicagotribune.com/history/ct-opinion-flashback-republican-party-origin-whigs-20210226-fkjz26k7vrbuhjpm5xaqefzgxa-story.html.

2   Ibid.

3   Michael Spencer, *Humanly Speaking: The Evil of Abortion, the Silence of the Church, and the Grace of God* (Colorado Springs, CO: Michael Spencer, 2021), 98.

4   Brian Kennedy and Courtney Johnson, "More Americans See Climate Change as a Priority, but Democrats Are much More Concerned Than Republicans," Pew Research, February 28, 2020, https://www.pewresearch.org/short-reads/2020/02/28/more-americans-see-climate-change-as-a-priority-but-democrats-are-much-more-concerned-than-republicans/.

5   Adam Andrzejewski, "Remembering 'Solyndra' – How Many $570M Green Energy Failures Are Hidden Inside Biden's Infrastructure Proposal?," *Forbes*, April 12, 2021, https://www.forbes.com/sites/adamandrzejewski/2021/04/12/remembering-solyndra—how-many-570m-green-energy-failures-are-hidden-inside-bidens-instructure-proposal/?sh=72e52d062672.

6   "Theodore Roosevelt and Conservation," National Park Services, https://www.nps.gov/thro/learn/historyculture/theodore-roosevelt-and-conservation.htm.

7   Dinah Voyles Pulver, "Cow Farts Are Bad for Earth, but Cow Burps Are Worse. New Plan Could Help Cows Belch Less," *USA Today*, September 22, 2023, https://www.usatoday.com/story/news/nation/2023/09/22/company-plans-to-solve-cow-burps-and-reduce-methane-emissions/70925187007/.

8   Dan Lashof, "5 Reasons the US Should Cut Its GHG Emissions in Half by 2030," World Resources Institute, February 24, 2021, https://www.wri.org/insights/5-reasons-us-should-cut-its-ghg-emissions-half-2030.

Chapter 10

1   James W. Keyes, TikTok, November 18, 2023, https://www.tiktok.com/t/ZPRvApBNY.

2   Wikipedia, "Combined U.S. Senate and House Time," https://en.wikipedia.org/wiki/List_of_members_of_the_United_States_Congress_by_longevity_of_service#Combined_U.S._Senate_and_U.S._House_time.

3   Geoffrey Skelly, "Congress Today Is Older Than It's Ever Been," FiveThirtyEight, April 3, 2023, https://fivethirtyeight.com/features/aging-congress-boomers/.

4   Zachary B. Wolf, "They're 80+. They're in Charge. They're Not Going Away," CNN, September 25, 2021, https://www.cnn.com/2021/09/25/politics/older-dc-politicians-what-matters/index.html.

5   Annie Karni, "Here Are the 20 Oldest Members of Congress," *New York Times*, September 8, 2023, https://www.nytimes.com/2023/09/08/us/politics/oldest-members-of-congress.html.

6   Stef. W. Knight, "Who's Been in Congress the Longest," Axios, March 13, 2022, https://www.axios.com/2022/03/13/longest-serving-members-congress.

7   Associated Press, "Voters to Choose between Rep. Sheila Jackson Lee and State Sen. John Whitmire for Houston Mayor," *Politico*, December 9, 2023, https://www.politico.com/news/2023/12/09/voters-to-choose-between-rep-sheila-jackson-lee-and-state-sen-john-whitmire-for-houston-mayor-00130942.

8   Aman Kidwai, "More Companies Are Setting Age Limits in Order to Retool Their Boards," *Fortune*, July 22, 2022, https://fortune.com/2022/07/22/more-companies-setting-age-limits-retool-diversity-makeup/.

9   Alberto Medina, Sara Suzuki, "41 Million Members of Gen Z Will Be Eligible to Vote in 2024," Tisch College, October 18, 2023, https://circle.tufts.edu/latest-research/41-million-members-gen-z-will-be-eligible-vote-2024.

10   "World Values Survey Wave 7 (2017–2022)," World Values Survey, https://www.worldvaluessurvey.org/WVSDocumentationWV7.jsp.

11   Ibid.

12   Learn more about US Term Limits at www.termlimits.com.

13   "Term Limits on Governor," US Term Limits, https://www.termlimits.com/governor_termlimits/.

14 "Tucker Amendments (August 18, 1789)," ConSource, https://www
.consource.org/document/tucker-amendments-1789–8-18/.

15 John F. Kennedy, "John F. Kennedy's Inaugural Address," John F.
Kennedy Presidential Library and Museum, January 20, 1961, https:
//www.jfklibrary.org/learn/education/teachers/curricular-resources
/ask-not-what-your-country-can-do-for-you#:~:text=Goals%
2FRationale-,John%20F.,way%20to%20the%20public%20good.

16 Ronald Reagan, "A Time for Choosing Speech," Ronald Reagan
Presidential Library & Museum, October 27, 1964, https://www
.reaganlibrary.gov/archives/speech/time-choosing-speech.

Chapter 11

1 Ronald Reagan, "Farewell Address to the Nation, January 11,
1989," Ronald Reagan Presidential Library & Museum, https:
//www.reaganlibrary.gov/archives/speech/farewell-address-nation
(accessed November 25, 2023).

2 Megan Brennan, "Extreme Pride in Being American Remains Near
Record Low," Gallup, June 29, 2023, https://news.gallup.com/poll
/507980/extreme-pride-american-remains-near-record-low.aspx.

3 Haadiza Ogwude, "'The World Has Been Watching': How a
Small Service at Asbury Took the Globe by Storm," *The Enquirer*,
February 27, 2023, https://www.cincinnati.com/story/news/2023/02
/27/how-asbury-university-revival-started-globe-by-storm
/69937478007/.